FILE UNDER ARCHITECTURE

The MIT Press
Cambridge, Massachusetts,
and London, England

FILE UNDER ARCHITECTURE
Herbert Muschamp

This book was printed and bound
by Clark-Franklin-Kingston Press Inc.
in the United States of America.

Library of Congress Cataloging in Publi-
cation Data
Muschamp, Herbert
  File under architecture.

  1.   Architecture.   I.   Title
NA2500.M83   720   74-3297
ISBN 0-262-13110-2

The author
gratefully
acknowledges
the kind
assistance of
Diane Peterson,
Hans Weilskov,
Henry Flesh,
Margot Doss,
Gail Rosenstock,
Sylvia Muschamp,
Gordon Stover,
Lloyd Kahn,
Edward Allen,
and
Robin Drake.

This book is dedicated to Gordon Baldwin
with special thanks and love.

FILE UNDER ARCHITECTURE

Architecture is a word.

Architecture is the kind of word subject
to so many interpretations on so many
different levels that it has utterly no
meaning out of context. Apart from its
use as a figure of speech, architecture
is worthless.

I am an architect who has neither
designed nor built any buildings nor has
the inclination to do so. I call myself
an architect purely out of the comic
conceit, which is all that remains of the
Western architectural tradition.
Buildings have such short life spans
nowadays, and few bother to look at
them, anyway. Planning schemes must be
revised each year and still can't keep
up. Last winter's cosmic-comical
conceptual designs are forgotten with
the appearance of the new spring line.
Books last longer, take up less space,
are easier to take care of, make better
gifts, than most buildings. In the last
analysis, architecture is not a very
highly evolved state of mind.

This book contains both history and
critique but is primarily neither. It is
intended as a monograph-in-words of my
recent work, a selection of material to
file under A for Architecture, along with
the records of other material efforts,
along with color slides of the pyramids,
snapshots of Notre Dame, Paxton's blot-
ting paper doodles for the Crystal
Palace, fabric swatches taken from
decorator renderings of model home
interiors, videotapes of vehicles
designed to support human life in outer
space. I am an architect without architecture, and this is my story.

Certainly, the role of architect has
interesting varieties of experience to
offer those who want to play it, but the
term Architecture - capital A - trans-
cends the scope of such specialized roles.
I could cite reasons why the Parthenon is
not valid as architecture, support the
proposition that pyromania is the only
pure form of architectural expression
left, point out the moral outrage of
funding extravagant building schemes
while men are starving next door. I could
devote this book to the argument that the

REAL ESTATE
MAKES MEN RICH

A city was built
at Pittsburgh,
Pa., because it
was the nerve
center of vast
coal fields.

A city was built
at St. Louis,
Mo., because it
was located on a
navigable river,
and had an inex-
haustible water
supply.

2

A city was built at Des Moines, Iowa, because it was located in the heart of great agricultural country.

A city was built at Wheeling, West Va., because natural gas furnished cheap fuel for manufacturing.

A city was built at Grand Rapids, Mich., because it was the market place for the vast timber forest of Michigan.

history of architecture is the record of its success as a means and its failure as an end; then write a sequel proving that the opposite is also true. I do not believe in the history of architecture.

Architecture needs no defense, no proof of validity, no art historian to interpret its value or place. Architecture requires no preservation committee nor reconstruction experts. Architecture requires no architects, no designers, no selection jury, no philosophy of design. Architecture requires all of these things. I do not believe in architecture.

The kind of architecture we trace back to Mesopotamia and came down to us through the Greeks via Pevsner has gone away and, when last heard from, was living near Orlando, Florida, under the auspices of the late Walt Disney. Its retirement was long overdue. A computer took over its job.

The architectural profession has steadily evolved into a watershed of twentieth-century arts and sciences, stealing visual images from all of them to create the

A city was built at Indianapolis because the great railroads of Indiana concentrated at that point.

A city was built at Kansas City because it was the home of a hustling, energetic, vigorous bunch of boosters who cut the word "fail" from their vocabulary and said "we will" and did.

A city was built at Chicago because of cheap freight rates and shipping facilities.

composite picture of a cultural disaster. To perpetuate the tired strains of its existence, architecture has reversed its purpose. When once it worked to establish the rational, ordered patterns by which civilization could be managed, it now works overtime to provide complex and contradictory chaos for a world machine in which order is determined by more sophisticated techniques. As the effectiveness of architecture as a space conditioner has been surpassed by that of later technologies, which do the job on a bigger scale, the stiff Western concept of architecture is transformed into a reconstructed museum dinosaur, graphic information without life, drawing board sonnets to ways of life foreclosed by nothing more horrifying than change.

When trains were invented, it was thought that humans could not survive speeds past forty miles per hour, and it was so: that which could not change died, or went to Florida to bide its time. There has been no completely satisfying architecture since the Industrial Revolution because after that time the concept of static space itself was no longer interesting, informative, or necessary. Since then one building has been just as good or bad as any other building. The fact that more building has been done since that time than had ever been done before, since the world began, merely helps diminish the premium attached to the quality of architectural space. The works of men like Paxton, Eiffel, and Fuller appear as time-to-time reminders, generally treated as novelty items and ignored as architecture, of the fact that we no longer need or want architecture to maintain our cultural equilibrium. Even later, when we recognize the achievement of these designers, when we accept them as the true builders of genius of their day and see the rest as just hacks or mandarins posing as radicals, we are still for the most part unable to use their designs organically, except perhaps as illustrations of the superfluousness of such knowing, correct solutions in our world of wheels, wires, and assorted times experienced without the need to believe in them. Consequently we have relied on men who were primarily nonbuilders

A city will be built at Muskogee because here we have accessible the coal of Pittsburgh; the water of St. Louis; the railroad of Indianapolis; the agriculture of Des Moines; the natural gas of Wheeling; the woods of Michigan; the hustling of Kansas City; and the cheap freight rates and shipping advantages of Chicago.

No Interest. No Taxes. Muskogee is destined to be the greatest city in the Southwest."

-John Thorpe

(Ruskin, Morris, Viollet-le-Duc, and
their heirs) to remind us that architecture still somehow matters.

The serious architect has spent many years
in training and feels entitled to his
traditional aura. He borrows images and
slogans from technology, politics, and
fashion but is appalled at the notion of
having to equate his work with these
sources. Thus it is fortunate that relatively few buildings are built by serious
architects and that we have a large
number of props other than buildings to
choose from in articulating the space we
inhabit.

My buildings wear Mona Lisa cufflinks. I
don't know any laws about what a window
wants to be, I know nothing about the
greater reality of the doorknob. Most of
what I know of the reflective qualities
of glass comes from watching my reflec-
tion in shop windows as I walk up fancy
streets.

My architecture follows me wherever I go;
I travel with a staple gun. The telephone
and radio make my architecture truly

6

THE ENVIRONMENTAL
KINEMATIC: A
MOVEMENT TOWARD
REALIZATION THAT
"MAN" AND HIS
ENVIRONMENT"
CANNOT BE
APPROACHED AS
SEPARABLE UNITS;
THAT DESIGN
EFFORTS BASED
UPON ANY
DISTINCTION
BETWEEN ONE
AND THE OTHER,
WITH OR WITHOUT
THE APPLIED
ORNAMENT OF
VERBAL ECOLOGY,
MUST PRODUCE
AS MUCH CHAOS
AS ORDER.

international. Every day I design a new link in my worldwide scheme to make myself feel at home in the world. Perhaps this is the principal motive behind all architecture. If so, I want my work to project this motive in its purest form, without the limitations imposed by walls and other unnecessary details. The god that used to dwell in those details is dead.

My architecture springs to life as I use it, when I use it; its success is determined by the degree to which I am able to use it; its colors, shapes, and forms by the ways in which I use it. My architecture is utterly polymorphous; it dissolves in time and distance. The light of the sun is but one of an infinite number of agents endlessly combining to radically alter my architecture, its meaning and essence, its beauty and ugliness. The reality of my architecture is the sum of the time and energy I dedicate to its experience.

When frost is on the windowpane, I might draw back the curtain. No architecture is as interesting as a stack of new maga-

zines on the floor of any room. In the
morning, all of Rome smells of coffee,
which isn't something that was cleverly
planned. While the means of architecture
may be measurable, the effects are
unforeseen. In London, the architectural
life is provided by pigeons; in
Washington, by arsonists. I once saw a
man trip on the steps leading up to the
Seagram Building plaza, the only three
steps in New York City, and he blew it;
the building teetered and collapsed in a
burst of post-Bauhaus slapstick.

The experience of architecture requires
no training, no special knowledge, no
trips to galleries, no admission tickets.
It is the only historic form which has
been continuously a public and a process
art. Open twenty-four hours a day,
architecture means opening doors, switch-
ing on lights, making noises, scanning
split-second flashes of blank wall, cleaning dust from the baseboards, swatting
roaches, watching ceilings peel and white
paint turn yellow - all the things you do
and events you witness in transforming

The kinematic
itself no
"real" solution,
except within the
strict confines
of the sensory.
Recession from
visual universe
beginning in
Renaissance
produced
cultural
apparatus
(the rational)
beyond the
sensory.
Progression of
consciousness
from sensory
to rational
to intuitive.

8

Kinesthetic
universe for
those who wish
to return
to world of
sensory phenomena.
Rational for
those who are
still trying
to get out.
Intuitive:
experience beyond
the sensory;
acceptance of
sensory experience
without desire to
articulate or
"reform" it;
sensory reform
regarded as
secondary
illusion.

the space you inhabit into the plausible
dimensions of day-to-day existence.

Since the rise of rapid technology and
the advent of democracy, the practicing
architect, despite claims and intentions,
has held no responsibility for the shape
of his own buildings apart from a thin
veneer. This helps to explain both the
rich stylistic confusion of nineteenth-
century architecture, which sought vainly
to regain the preeminence of architecture
in the cultural hierarchy by the start-
ling use of heavy bombastic ornament, and
also the stylized plainness or brutalism
of early to mid-twentieth-century design,
which exploited the shock value of the
opposite extreme to reach the same goal -
regained preeminence - but again without
success.

This also explains why the strongest work
done by specialized architects in the
past two centuries has been fantastic or
visionary architecture. Beginning in
France with Boullée and Ledoux, and
continuing up to the present, certain

Sensory universe:
for the
99.98 percent
of the population
who want
to be happy,
be entertained,
have a good time,
be told
what to do.
Rational
universe:
for .019 percent
who want to have
an unhappy time
and tell others
what to do.
Intuitive
universe:
for .001 percent
who are
interested
in neither good
nor bad times
nor telling
nor being told
what to do;
who,
like sensory
group,
are interested
in experience
rather than
analysis
but who,
unlike sensory
group,
seek primarily
only the
experience
which bypasses
all the senses.

architects have detected this shifting
of roles in the cultural fabric, and its
implications for architecture. These
artists have understood that the preservation of architecture as an art form
depends upon the creation of cerebral
artifacts, the design of buildings which
will not or cannot be built. Only in this
way can architectural work continue to be
subject to the terms of the artist. Thus
it was that the Bauhaus produced many
interesting teachers and exciting design
ideas but failed to build a house other
than its own. Hence also the bitter
frustration of architects like
Le Corbusier (an artist who in his
earlier years had flourished as a painter
and visionary), whose buildings failed to
end wars and wipe out mal de siecle for
the simple reason that no static solution,
no matter how beautiful, could incarnate
the dreams of the new spirit for which
he offered Greek atavistic answers.
Failing to comprehend that the world was
big enough to include both the noble
ruins of the Parthenon and the honky-tonk
of Forty-second Street, he staged heroic
play-offs between the two and raged as
each match came off a draw.

10

Manifestations of
architecture:

Sensory:
the beautiful
building build-
ing, its creation
and destruction,
long-range
fashion

Rational:
the design
philosophy, the
high ideal,
utopias within
grasp, reform
through design

Intuitive:
internalized,
unpremeditated
response,
divining-rod
sense, walking
through walls,
respecting the
rights of others
to have them,
working on
eliminating
one's own need
for them.

The shape of architecture had already
fallen under the direct aesthetic control
of masses of unknown, unknowable people:
subway riders, crowds in Times Square on
New Year's Eve, Levittowners with their
lawns, shop owners with their precious
square feet of street frontage, blacks
with their transistor radios, Sunday
America cutting out on the highway with
somewhere else to go. Architects preach-
ing corny sermons about a democratic
architecture had been hiding their heads
in the Mediterranean sand too long. A
democratic architecture was already alive
and flourishing - only it wasn't to be
controlled by classically inclined
architects but by consumers themselves
and those interested in exploiting them.
The only thing left for most architects
to do was to crank out endless drawings
and find other ways to occupy themselves
in a handicap career.

The only thing left for Western architecture itself to do was to go farther west
to southern California and die just like
the earlier dinosaurs who met an equally
tacky demise in the tar pits of La Brea.
All the many ways in which space could be

11

articulated as isolated parcels were used
up, burned out, and shipped out for prefab
emergency use in the used car lot of
architecture on the West Coast.

The story of how European architecture
arrived in America, and was dragged across
the continent to California, a place of
death and metamorphosis, is the real story
of modern architecture, though it lacks
the seal of professional approval. The
orthodox version cites Chicago as the
place in America where modern architecture
became a tangible reality, and this is so.
But it is not the buildings of Adler,
Sullivan, and Wright that justify the
claim. These men worked too firmly within
the traditional European value system of
logical design and sensible artistic expression to come up with anything original. It was the White City, the Chicago
Columbia Exposition of 1893 - exactly
what these architects despised so much -
that demonstrated the direction of an
architectural sensibility so revolutionary that it took fifty years before its
significance was understood. Sullivan,
with a European-trained perception that
took him no further than the plaster

ARCHITECTURE
AS
PRIMARY
HEROIC SYMBOL
OF PROCESS
OF ILLUSION-
MAKING WITHIN
VISUAL
FRAMEWORK,
THE
ARCHITECTURAL
STATEMENT:
SYMBOLIC
INTERPENETRA-
TION
BETWEEN
REALITY AND
ILLUSION:
"WE BESEECH
YOU
TO RESPECT
OUR WALL,
AND WHAT IT
MEANS TO US...."
SANCTITY
OF THE
PRIVILEGE
TO SUPPORT
A GROUP
OF THESE
COLLECTIVE
ILLUSIONS
FOR THE
MAKE-BELIEVE
BENEFIT
OF ALL.

Beaux Arts facades of the White City,
missed the point entirely and charged
that the exposition had set back the cause
of modern architecture half a century. In
fact, the exposition was an early instance
of an unprecedented, truly modern attitude
toward design. Architecture had been
handed to the people. It was an artistic
failure, but its implications went way
beyond the narrow traditional systems
used to evaluate art. People loved it.
In the White City it was discovered that,
for the new public that architecture was
coming to serve, having a good time was
more important than good taste. Style was
truly irrelevant, occasion alone mattered.
It was demonstrated for the first time on
a large scale that faking it was a valid
architectural method; that plaster could
be dressed up as stone to enhance the
sense of event, the process of occasion;
that a temporary structure had just as
much meaning as one designed for longer
use, and that it didn't have to look
temporary to be a success. Architects were
no longer responsible for the success or
failure of buildings. From now on, form
would follow fiction. A new aesthetic was
born, but architects failed to see it,

13

The classic
first-year
design school
question:
How much is man
influenced by,
and how much
does he
influence,
his environment?
A: He is
influenced
100 percent;
he influences
100 percent;
neither has
any influence.
He is influenced,
for those who
want to be told
what to do.
He influences,
for those
who want
to tell others
what to do.
There is no
interchange,
for those
who refuse
to recognize
that environment
has any
external reality
beyond
its ability
to provide
that reality
for those
who need it.

just as, four decades earlier, they had
refused to recognize the Crystal Palace
as architecture at all. Recognition of
the new architecture would have to wait
until it was transplated to the virgin,
relatively un-Europeanized soil under the
expanding California bell jar, where it
took root and grew too impossibly big to
ignore.

The elements of this aesthetic had been
present since colonial days, but America
was a nation of immigrant riffraff
snobbishly engaged in the common destruction of a rich variety of European
vernacular traditions, a practice that
prevented them from recognizing for many
generations the true character of the new
culture they were creating in the process.
Everybody was learning to dance the
gavotte and to bow and curtsy like little
ladies and gents. In the classy burial
grounds of Europe, America went shopping
for necrocosmetics with which to mask the
humble origins. Dignity and respectability
were at the top of the list, and back
bounced Rome to set the style of the new
pomp culture. Naturally, the living

14

culture of the Indians had to be
eliminated; dead languages were the most
important subjects in school. Tepees were
no good for this type of glory - surely
the Greco-Roman temple was the only true
interpretation of physical space a
civilization could possess.

AS ARCHITECTURE
TURNS TO RUINS,
GREATEST PROBLEMS
NEVER SOLVED,
ONLY OUTGROWN.

People who had nothing before were suddenly in possession of an immense new
world; they could do with it whatever
they pleased. What would later come to be
called the California aesthetic began
right then and there, in the sudden city of
Washington, D.C., for example: where
M. L'Enfant came from Paris to set up,
for the new, instant elite, a short-order
European capitol with quick plazas and a
side order of statues to go. Long before
holograms, TV studios, and MacDonald's
Golden Arches, men were learning to use
architecture as a prefabricated kit of
parts with which to fracture and reset
parcels of space instantly, as occasion
demanded.

The bulldozer, wrecker's ball, and
related tools have always contributed the

ARCHITECTURE
AS VESTIGE
OF PURITAN ETHIC
(THE DEVIL
FINDS WORK FOR
IDLE HANDS).
"THE
HARDEST TIME
IN A COMMUNE,
PARTICULARLY
DROP CITY,
IS THE TIME
AFTER THE
BUILDING
GETS DONE.
WHILE EVERYONE
IS WORKING
TOGETHER
ON ACTUAL
CONSTRUCTION
THE ENERGY
IS CENTERED,
THERE IS
FANTASTIC
HIGH SPIRIT,
EVERYONE KNOWS
WHAT HE IS DOING
ALL THE TIME.
BUT AFTER THE
BUILDING
IS DONE
COMES A TIME
OF DISSOLUTION.

prime ingredients of American architecture; the buildings themselves could have been made of papier-mâché. That they stood up as long as they did was generally more an economic inconvenience than a standing invitation to ponder the timeless essence of American civilization. Of course the buildings in Washington, D.C., have had to stay up for the benefit of junior high field trips. They have no other reason to exist; they are no more than 3-D postcards set up on Ektachrome lawns under Kodak skies, connected by purple velvet covered ropes, forming a ready-made backdrop to memorialize against. The reality of this architecture lies not in the stone but in the electrons duplicating its image on TV screens all over the world. Its essence is illusion, unlike that of cities such as medieval Baghdad and nineteenth-century Paris, where the decisions of civic planning were determined by the concrete nature of military tactics in the event of political disturbance. The architecture of Americans supplied cerebral props rather than the physical tools required by earlier civilizations to maintain the status quo.

16

THERE'S NO FOCUS FOR GROUP ENERGY, AND MOST HIPPIES JUST DON'T HAVE ANYTHING TO DO WITH THEIR INDIVIDUAL ENERGY..." (PETER RABBIT, DROP CITY)... NOR DO MOST OTHER PEOPLE. CHRISTIANITY DECLINING AFTER THE BUILDING OF CATHEDRALS, GREECE SLIPPING AFTER THE GOLDEN AGE, MAYAN CITIES DESERTED, ETC. HEROIC EXTERNALIZING. NO MEANING APART FROM ENERGY PUT INTO IT BY INDIVIDUALS. NOT A SOLUTION AS END RESULT, JUST SOLUTION OF KEEPING BUSY.

The business of Americans was a glamorous destiny to be made manifest as soon as possible. There was no time to fritter away on the old up-and-down creative cycle; anything that did not point up-and-up had been declared unconstitutional. Since architecture could not always be relied upon to do this, at least not fast enough, the business of shaping the environment was handed over to other specialists: to Benjamin Franklin and his stove and lightning rod, Fulton and the Folly, the riders of the pony express, Morse and the telegraph, Edison and the light bulb, Bell and the telephone, the Wright brothers, and so on. These men provided the genius by which the official up-and-up doctrine could be realistically carried out.

Architecture required no genius. It required nothing more than a catalog of quickly available parts and the manpower to set them up. This casual, unselfconscious artlessness formed the basis of the American vernacular, and by the time Americans came to develop the state of California the vernacular was an estab-

17

lished tradition. The retirement hobby of
Hadrian (who collected scale models of all
the ancient world's best buildings for his
villa in Capri) had become the life-style
of millions. The wonders of the world of
architecture were set up in multiple
editions, with Fair Deal mortgage terms
for all. And why not? If, in your twentieth-century lifetime, you could afford a
nice Palladian villa, a temple of Vesta,
a wee thatched country cottage o' the
kirk, an ivy-covered cloister, a Spanish
hacienda, an exotic pink pagoda in dragons
and gold, a Tudor mansion, a Taj Mahal,
and all immaculately landscaped and
appointed, all equally magnificent under
the light of both the sun and tastefully
recessed lighting fixtures.

From the very beginning, everything made
in California was more specialized, more
highly fragmented, more separate and
apart than anywhere else on earth. There
was not even an attempt at uniformity,
and the result was that everything was so
isolated from and unrelated to everything
else, every house was so unique and
separate that there was no way to get
from one place to the next so they had to

run strips of highway and neon to connect
it all, and, being bigger, brighter, and
more obvious, the connections became the
architecture - everything else was just a
blur in passing, and the architecture
became more uniform than any architecture
had been for thousands of years.

The hill of Universal City studios rises
above Los Angeles, a symbolic new world
Acropolis. No one lives in the Universal
City; it is a place of ghosts, dreams, and
the making of them. It is a machine of

Great affirma-
tions of belief
in the strength
of mankind for
times when
spirits are low
(Rockefeller
Center in the
depression).

substitute environments: sets stacked up
like books, warehouses full of candle-
sticks and dummy staircases, feathers,
bogus walls and cardboard antiques, back-
less houses and painted poplar-lined
avenues. The experienced cameraman can
make it real, bring it to life. Rome was
not built in a day, but Universal City
could mock one up in an hour.

Studios have shut down because we no
longer need them; we have already learned
from them how to make reality out of
fiction. That this is at best a temporary
reality is the essential advantage over
previous architectural aesthetics in con-

19

forming to the rapidly changing needs of
individuals. In a system designed to answer
the wants of millions of separately evolv-
ing people, the emphasis is not on
permanent solutions but on the routes of
access to potential realities and the
means with which to shape them. The studio
movie, by encouraging unprecedented numbers
of people to practice the willing suspen-
sion of disbelief in environmental ab-
stractions, was the first medium to exploit
these possibilities in an interface with
the visual cues of conventional architecture. Thus it was later possible for
Fellini to film on location in Rome and
make the real city look fake: the Eternal
City is recast in the image of the
Universal City, a town of tourists and
movie stars, a place where nobody lives.

DROP CITY:
ON THE ONE HAND:
ALL THOSE GREAT
MELLOW TIMES,
FELLOWSHIP, UNITY,
BROTHERHOOD,
"THESE ARE MY
PEOPLE" FEELINGS;
ON THE OTHER:
THAT THESE
FEELINGS ARE
ILLUSIONS QUICKLY
TURNING TO THEIR
OPPOSITES...
WONDERFUL IF
APPRECIATED FOR
THEIR FLEETING-
NESS - A
NIGHTMARE IF
REGARDED AS A
FOUNDATION FOR
"SOMETHING
BEYOND."

The Universal City exploded what was left
of the old architectural dimensions after
rapid technology and middle-class affluence had laid the groundwork of the new
sensibility. To live in a palace was now
every man's birthright, and the Universal
City showed how to make it come true -
not by erecting new Blenheims and Bucking-

hams, but by designing cybernetic systems
of environmental control in which the
individual man held the responsibility for
programming his own passage through space.
Specialized architecture, by steadfastly
refusing to surrender this responsibility
to all, impeded this process. Various last-
ditch attempts (such as De Stijl in early
and Total Design in mid-twentieth century)
were formulated by architects to offset it,
thus isolating their activities still
further from the course of events.

Revenge was sought through the creation
of city planning, but it was too late.
The new aesthetic was already reinforced
by a number of new media in which
twentieth-century men were enthusiastical-
ly participating. Like it or not, the
parallel lines of once isolated cultures
had already met in the dreamtime lounges
of Orly, Heathrow, Kennedy, da Vinci, and
O'Hare. The new architecture flew over
the tops of the tallest buildings and
looking down it was impossible to tell
whether they were made of timber or of
steel, and up there it didn't matter much,
anyway. You couldn't go home again, for

the simple reason that you could no longer leave it in the first place. The architectural matrix of man had shifted from the medieval image of the city to the individual process of making connections, between cities, between rooms, between times and distances imaginatively synthesized. Boeing and Pan Am provided the new architectural goods and services that construction firms were unable to supply. Walls had told their story.

The CIAM architects sensed this, expanded the scope of their visions accordingly, but would not acknowledge the obvious consequences: that the shaping of architecture devolved on materials and methods wholly outside the grasp of the CIAM grid. The creation of the curtain wall was a nice try, but all walls, whether structural or nonstructural, had lost their symbolic meaning. The CIAM architects attempted to posit real buildings within ideal, imaginary grand designs and failed because they ignored the networks that were already in operation.. Those who succeeded were the builders who simply

In the word architecture itself: necessary acceptance of it as no more than illusion, belief in the meaning of the universal "beyond" above texture, symbolism of a greater reality. The architect makes texture; people make architecture. Walt Whitman: "All architecture is what you do to it when you look upon it."

22

Unquestioned,
taken-for-
granted belief,
that makes
tecture
architecture,
like green
glasses worn
by the inhab-
itants of Oz.

Thing from
Anaïs Nin's
diary
about the
transformation
of
Henry Miller's
room
in Paris,
as he prepared
to move out
of it:
cracks and stains
becoming
more visible,
the ceiling
appearing
to sag.

accepted buildings as static short-term
solutions and went on to develop as real
estate the junction points (suburbs,
shopping centers, airports) of the new
architecture as they were gradually being
defined by other, more dynamic media.
Builders such as Levitt, Hilton and
Lefrak arrived at these solutions while
modern architects devised complex paper
theories to prove to themselves that (by
calling a house a machine, for example) a
blueprint product could be just as
exciting as a plane ride.

Despite the high-sounding humanitarian
jargon used to launch these theories in
public, the motivational history of
modern architecture is depressingly bald
in its bitter pettiness. In the best-for-
less rough concrete and exposed electrical
circuitry of brutalism, for example, one
can easily detect the arrogant distaste
with which the displaced mandarin, compelled by changing social pressures,
places his talent at the disposal of the
masses; read the physical projection of
frustrated totalitarian values that the

public had best adjust to, under penalty
of having to live without the redeeming
social value of high art.

In professional journals, editorial
opinion tried for solidarity ("We, the
undersigned architects...") but generally
opted for morbid hysteria ("Is Architecture Dead?") in the struggle to secure a
permanent place for the noblest art of
elitest control within a modern sensibility which had declared such attitudes inar-
tistic, if not obsolete. The academic
dream of modern architecture died when it
became apparent that some one way of looking at things was not sufficient to support the rich realities of imagined existence, that so much was occurring everywhere on so many different levels that no
immaculate conception of how the world
should be was even worth the fanfare, much
much less its weight in stone. The cathedrals were not white, they were dirty,
and no amount of theoretical sandblasting
could restore the expired perceptual patterns that had created them. Less was
more, but not enough. The only manifesto
that could be written would have to be
rewritten a million times a minute; not

Design as
would-be thief
of spontaneity.
Designed
spontaneity -
doublespeak
conceit.
Greater control -
greater outburst
of chaos.
The bomb as
autopunishment
for increased
control over
universal
environment.

24

Design as
process seeking
to serve
human experience
by containing it
well,
thereby going
on the assumption
that
this experience
can be
so contained.
Successful design
successfully
containing
even the
processes of
the obliteration
of containment.
Gothic cathedral
charged with
ritual energy
as a symbol of
escape route
from horror of
contemporary
life.
When building
was done
anonymously
...and
no one
thought of
not building...
the arch,
still having
the power of
the miraculous,
because it
had not been
done before;
an architecture
worthy of
the experience
of unity.

even Corb had that kind of energy. The
critics held fast to the story that all
great art was the product of an elite.
Everybody else went out to the movies.

Mies van der Rohe's Barcelona pavilion
was one of the last major works of
architecture to succeed on the basis of
visual aesthetics. Mies was able to get
away with this not only because the work
was visually beautiful but also, and
more importantly, because it met the
demands (not yet recognized as such) of
the new architectural sensibility. It was
an almost purely imaginary building; it
had both the source and the effect of the
true myth. It stood erect for just a few
months, was carefully recorded in photo-
graphs, then was disassembled almost immediately. It left the Barcelona table
and chair behind as souvenirs to be used
later on in connecting some of the tritest,
most unimaginative spaces with a mythical
space that was remembered as breathtaking.
It captured the imagination of those
seeking confirmation of the hope that
modern architects might not have to
compromise their oligarchic politics in
order to impress the public with the

striking good looks of their architecture. For those who believed that a building was still viable as a space conditioner, the Barcelona pavilion became a token of proof.

Trying to inhabit such a symbol was altogether a different matter. Dr. Farnsworth, who commissioned her friend Mies to build her a similar pavilion outside Chicago, tried and failed. While her house bore the scrutiny of Ezra Stoller's camera with supreme grace and style, it failed to provide a home, and the inflexibility of its design prevented her from making it one.

DESIGN AND STAGNATION, TWO HALVES OF THE SAME THING. A THING PERCEIVED AS EXTERNAL: ALWAYS GOING BOTH WAYS, ENDLESSLY, WITHOUT EVER GETTING ANYWHERE. MOVING FORWARD IN A SERIES OF VERY ATTRACTIVE FRAUDS. THE HISTORY OF ARCHITECTURE: TO PICK OUT THOSE ELEMENTS WHICH SEEM TO HAVE EVOLVED SOMETHING TOWARD SOMETHING BETTER.

Poor Edith. She expressed her dissatisfaction publicly, and that was her mistake. She had hurt the cause and must be punished. Word was passed round from drawing board to lecture hall that she had made improper advances to Mies, that she had been rejected, that this was the cause of her disillusion with the modern movement. The story is worth telling only because it reflects so accurately the professional sentiment (which at the time ran very high) that architecture is such

26

Through symbols,
man seeks
to express,
rather than
contain,
his totality.
Yet
(breathing in,
breathing out)
the symbol
itself
becomes a
barrier,
a wall,
a screen against
this totality.
In architecture:
there is
no Gothic
or Romanesque
style,
nor any style,
until the
nineteenth
century
when all walls
ceased to have
symbolism.
Then,
you could have
any style
you wanted
(just as,
by the time the
Greeks came to
catalog the
auditory
universe,
the ancient
musical modes
had lost their
symbolism).

a noble thing to do that efforts on its
behalf must be beyond reproach, if not
beyond laughter at the spectacle of those
who took the modern movement so seriously
that they consciously attempted to live
like machines.

In expanding the scope of architecture
beyond buildings to embrace every method
used to make home out of space, due emphasis must now be placed on statistics,
intentions, and motivational energy
formerly classed as irrelevant to the
work of artists. Environments collect all
the garbage we drop when we think no one
is looking. To those trained to regard
architecture as the highest expression of
human art, it comes as a shock to find,
reflected in the manmade environment, the
full range of human motives, from the
highest down to the most ignoble. Only a
fool would try to separate the architecture done with an eye to aesthetic appeal
from that done for other reasons, for
history judges differently, even if art
historians don't.

President Nixon declared that America must
have good architecture because a civiliza-

ARCHITECTURE
AS A SCREEN
AGAINST THE
POSSIBLE:
WHEN YOU ERECT
A WALL OF
TEN FEET
YOU ARE DENYING
THE POSSIBILITY
OF A WALL
OF NINE OR
ELEVEN FEET,
THE POSSIBILITY
OF NO WALL
AT ALL.
WHEN YOU TURN
A BLANK WALL
TO THE STREET,
YOU DENY THE
POSSIBILITY
OF A VISION OF
THE STREET
FROM WITHIN,
THE POSSIBILITY
OF REFLECTIONS
FOR PEDESTRIANS,
OF GLIMPSES
OF LIGHT WITHIN,
ETC.

tion is usually judged on the basis of its architectural relics, but only a tyrant or a vulgarian would try to impress history, and anyone who has ever stepped out of his car and taken a short walk beneath the concrete pylons of a superhighway knows precisely on what material the judgment of visually oriented historians will be based anyway, despite all the hype, all the Record House of the Year awards, all the glamour surrounding the dedication ceremonies of our official entries in the cultural sweepstakes. In time capsules under the earth we bury all the trinkets we like best, but we also bury stockpiles of napalm and nerve gas in monuments to motives time will not conceal.

The character of our architecture is shaped by circumstances and events that drawing board decisions can neither control nor mask. For example, after World War II, the United States Congress declared as national policy the intention "to provide a decent home and a suitable living environment for every American" - a policy reavowed in 1968. Entirely apart from the many questions raised as to what

28

WHEN YOU PLACE
ONE WINDOW
ON THE STREET,
YOU DENY
THE POSSIBILITY
OF TWO WINDOWS,
NO WINDOWS,
A GLASS WALL.
THE DOME
CEASELESSLY
EXPRESSES
ITS DOMENESS,
THE RIGHT ANGLE
ITS RIGHT
ANGULARITY;
THE BUILDING
TOWERS
OVER ONE'S HEAD
NO MATTER
WHAT THE WEATHER
UNLESS ONE FLIES
BY IN A PLANE.
THE POINT IS
NOT TO STOP
MAKING WALLS,
BUT TO
RECOGNIZE THEM
IN THEIR
ARBITRARY COAT
OF FANCY.

constitutes a suitable living environment, these intentions and the motives behind them are alone sufficient to transform the perceptible environment into a picture no architect could ever render into the kind of art his training has taught him to produce. No matter - if the motives are strong enough, someone will figure out how to do it.

The motives that created the postwar housing industry were potent indeed; the primary goal of the government was to ease the United States out of an economic slump by generating new sources of capital. To provide this goal with a healthy moral pretext, the ugly issues of ghetto living were exploited along with the good intentions of Eleanor Roosevelt in a manner which suggested that the act of building was a solution to pressing social problems. Politicians are at least as notorious as architects in failing to comprehend how an idea that looked good on paper will fail to make it on the street.

In 1969 the Secretary of Housing and Urban Development (not an architect, a

Artaud
crouching
in the corner;
shattering
intended
architectural
perspective,
how a thing
is to be seen.

planner, or even a builder, but an auto-
mobile manufacturer) announced Project
Breakthrough, a program that "must deal
with two related problems. First is the
creation of housing production in large
volume.... Second is assuring the availa-
bility of markets to absorb the increased
volume of housing production." In other
words, even if more building were not in
demand, it would be necessary to create
that demand, despite the ready availabil-
ity of more sophisticated solutions to
these problems, such as the pill.

By 1970 the A.M. easy-listening radio
stations were flooded with government ads
that sounded like aspirin commercials:
"Oh, George, I just can't stand it any
more!" "Honey, take an aspirin...." "I
don't need an aspirin, I need a new house!
I'm sick of this cramped apartment, and
with another baby coming...." "Oh, are
you going to start in on that again? What
sort of house could I get on my eighty
bucks a week?" "Well, George, with an
FHA-assisted loan...." The implications of
this approach to the environmental welfare
of individuals (that building cures head-
aches, that people should expect new

ARCHITECTURE
AS SCREEN
AGAINST
PERCEPTION
OF UNITY;
AS ANTICATHEDRAL,
SYMBOL
OF SEPARATION
RATHER THAN
COMMUNION.

30

building, that there is unlimited space
for building for ever-increasing population, that housing units are more important than communities) completely revolutionize both the visual aesthetics and
the social structure of environments long
before architects are even called in for
advice.

The visual statement of the superhighway
was made in much the same fashion.
Obviously cars and highways were never
the most elegant solution to the problem
of mass transportation. However, as
Detroit lobbyists argued successfully in
Washington for many years, they comprised
the only solution that would both serve
the needs of individuals and support the
United States economic growth rate as
well. The building of a highway system
encouraged the folks to buy cars, and to
travel, even if they previously had no
special desire to do so.

Route H-1 interstate highway in Hawaii
costs six hundred million dollars, is
twenty-four miles of road going so far
nowhere, but provides salaries for a
Hawaiian highway commission and work for

BUILDING
AS SYMBOL OF
BREAKDOWN;
RUIN,
OF
REINTEGRATION.

31

Flaunting
Teilhard
de Chardin
as a
divinely
inspired
excuse for
indefinitely
postponing the
Omega Point;
which,
since it
can know
no beginning
and no end,
cannot possibly
be any more
in the future
than it is
in the
present.
Reform by
design as
technique of
postponing
having
to give up
quest for
knowledge
as the
ultimate task
of men;
refusal to
admit that
knowledge
does no more
than replace
old illusions
with new ones,

builders and will ultimately transform
the environment into its own justifica-
tion, carrying the American pop art
highway aesthetic to the fiftieth state
just like the missionaries took the
Bible there over a century ago. The gas
stations and Howard Johnsons could all be
replicas of the Barcelona pavilion, but
even at reduced energy crisis speeds it
wouldn't make much difference.

In the Team 10 Primer somebody says,
"Mies is great but Corb communicates,"
and there's no doubt about that. Charles
Jeanneret was a still-life painter who
felt that in order to become the architect he wanted to be, he had to change his
name to Le Corbusier - and here we have
the first of many clues in Corb's work to
understanding why current architectural
trends follow such schizoid patterns. It
is difficult to believe that one man
could have accomplished so much,
especially since he didn't accomplish
anything he set out to do - except that
while there were modern architects before
him there was no modern architecture. He
invented it, and it is easy to forget how
many ideas, many of them still regarded

32

having
greater value
only within
the narrow
limitations
observed
within the
narrow
illusion
of linear
progress.
Again,
that a thing
means more
than what
it is,
beyond its
artificially
fortified
context.
Also:
the sad
assumption
that
communication
is a
struggle
rather than
a miracle.
Refusal
to admit that
the experience
of unity
cannot be
directly
communicated.

in some circles as advanced, originated with his energy.

He wanted to do everything and to know all things so that he could build for all men, so that he could be of the stature he imagined the Greeks had possessed, but he was Swiss at a time when it was much better to be an American if you wanted to do that sort of thing. He hated being Swiss, he called them a nation of watch-makers, and he had contempt for Europeans in general because they lived in and around old buildings and didn't seem to mind it that much. He compared them to donkeys because their cities had curved and crooked streets. He loved Americans at first because they seemed so healthy and had so much technology to toss around, but his affection was not returned because he was such a talker, and the Americans he tried to consort with were not artists but corporation men who were a bit suspici-ous of talkers and poets. He grew sour on everyone.

Corb was a visual pantheist, that is to say he didn't know anything at all about natural ecosystems except that they were

33

all very beautiful to look at. He was
particularly obsessed with the sun because
the sun was such a potent factor in the
life of the Mediterranean countries where
the purest classical architecture had
been done, where dazzling relics gave life
to a soaring vision of healthy bodies,
sound minds, and tragically high ideals.

Thus intoxicated, Corb veered off toward
an architecture everybody else was happy
to be getting away from. By communicating
his architectural reveries in terms of a
verbose humanitarian doctrine made up of
parts lifted from assorted political
manifestoes (revolutionary Russian,
American, and French), Corb tried to
present buildings as the twentieth-century
panacea, the medium in which nature, man,
his ideologies and technologies could be
permanently reconciled.

At a time when every individual did not
yet possess a car and a radio, and smog
was not yet a major political issue, this
poetic vision did not seem entirely naive.
Nature was still a more or less abstract
quantity, technology was the reasonable
exploitation of physical truths to set

34

man free from material concerns, progress
(including political progress) was still
our most important product. Yet while his
writings contained these elements successfully within the framework of a nicely
balanced obsession, his buildings were
only buildings and did not speak so
poetically. The vision could be maintained
cerebrally, but not supported on concrete
pilotis. Private patrons and sympatheti-
cally inclined artists could participate
in his struggle, but the public at large
saw only the crude walls, at best recalled his famous inflammatory statements
like "Machine for living," "The New York
skyscrapers aren't tall enough," "Suburbs
are a menace," without being aware of the
pattern that gave these elements their
meaning, and Corb didn't want to build
for just a handful of friends like
Tristan Tzara and the Steins, the
Parisian cognoscenti who knew his work
well, read his issues of L'Esprit Nouveau
on art and exercise, collected his purist
paintings. He wanted to build for the
great new masses of democracy and/or
socialism, and these people, even most of
those who inhabited his public buildings,
had no idea what was going on. To them

35

the Modulor, the human measure by which all of Corb's architectural dimensions were determined, was, if anything, no more than an excuse for a nice piece of sculptural relief at the base of the housing blocks, a bit of urban art essentially no different from something you could get Lipschitz, Picasso, or the WPA to do. Published artistic intentions were of little value in the homes of people who showed little aptitude and less interest in assimilating such ideas.

In the fifties, Corb went to India to scatter the remains of his vital ambitions over a land he was too old to understand, a country deep in the throes of cold turkey following British withdrawal, where his brand of cultural aggression was the last thing needed. He was much sadder now than when he voyaged to the New World, but no weaker in the faith that his own enthusiasm for architectural form gave this form the power to change basic patterns of life, to unite (in this case) people who had little enough in common with each other and next to nothing in common with him, people in whose lives

Einstein did not make application to the patent office, as Fuller did. He did not aspire to be a comprehensive verbal god, did not need to coin clever portmanteau words to drum up publicity. By confining his speech to the most abstract language available, pure mathematics, he obtained the experience of the universe (of unity) having no possibility of external application.

36

There is
nothing
to carry away,
bring back,
from this
experience,
but shadows
(E = mc²),
and the
shadow of
shadows -
crass toy
models
of the
universe
to be
peddled in
bazaars
(batteries
not included).
There is
no geodesic
city
without the
hydrogen bomb.
Utopia
is
Oblivion.

Greek glory and United States technology were of no more significance than Queen Victoria's bun had been in the lives of their grandparents a century before. The only Indians who sought these things were the European-educated bureaucrats, petty civil service status seekers who loathed the churlish Indian peasants in any case and weren't exactly looking forward to being stuck in some obscure provincial capital. Having the famous French architect design it would provide some compensation, however (like wearing a Paris original - say a Saint Laurent bush jacket - on a sweaty African safari), and they knew they wouldn't have to pay him very much because he was desperate to do some real city planning before he died.

Chandigarh, in short, was no great plum - a bare notch or two above the great Haitian capital of Duvalierville. But Corb had missed out on Brasilia and the others and they'd even disowned him at the United Nations headquarters, so he jumped at the chance. He flew out to India with his bundle of Cartesian tricks and a group of devotees, drove out to the center of

Fuller's
Dymaxion car
in fatal
accident
on its first
exhibition
trial run.
While it was
"The other
driver's"
fault,
the incident
perfectly
typifies
the way
all utopian
designs fail
by failing
to consider
at least one-
half of the
forces
operative in
human
experience
(for example,
"evil"
politicians
recklessly
speeding by
in limousines).
No blame.

a flat plain in the Punjab where no one
had ever shown any interest to live,
planted his flag, set up his office on
the site. He made drawings for a city, a
social organism bound by his walls and
terms - and this was in a country that had
gone to great lengths to drive out
Europeans, a country that already had the
ghost of a European city set up at New
Delhi by Lutyens, with a two-mile
boulevard and much Victorian pomposity,
architecture coming right out of the
nineteenth-century imperial tradition,
which had made instant classics out of
everything by Kipling. Since Corb worked
well within this tradition, he was safe
from all pressures to try to understand
the complexities of Indian civilization,
its attitudes toward the land, toward
habitation, and the sources of this
cultural orientation. No, he was merely
displeased that India was such a backward
place; that there could be no elevators
and therefore no tall buildings; that
there could be no air conditioning, none
of the respiration exacte he had pre-
scribed for his ideal, imaginary,
hermetically sealed buildings all over

38

"The foxes
have holes,
and the birds
of the air
have nests;
but the
Son of Man
hath not
where to lay
his head."

THROWN OUT
OF THE
FORD
FOUNDATION
BUILDING
FOR TRYING
TO SIT DOWN
BENEATH A
TREE
AND EAT MY
LUNCH THERE.
SITTING IN
PALEY PARK:
THE ONLY TIME
I'VE EVER BEEN
FRIGHTENED BY
NEW YORK CITY
TRAFFIC.

the earth. Indians and Pakistanis fought, starved, moved from place to place as Corb worked to define the axis of his architecture, wondered where to put the windows, what colors to paint the columns, and whether or not to use electronic amplification in the council assembly chamber.

And then, when the major buildings of the civic center at Chandigarh were near completion and the rest of the town had been gridded out, and they were starting work on the strictly class-separated housing, when they had laid out all the arbitrary axis boulevards and the great dustbin plazas, and the architects were all sitting around one evening in the midst of it, and it was obvious that the enterprise was a failure, one of the associate architects, Jane Drew, perhaps just out of embarrassment, said to Corb: "Why don't you erect monuments in the center of the city of Chandigarh which express your philosophy and the relation-ship of your architecture to nature?" and they were ready to jump at any straw at that point, so in heroic concrete

39

Corb made monoliths of all the great
intentions that had failed: the cycle of
the sun, the open hand, the human figure
of the Modulor - symbols of those noble
elements that had not come across in the
buildings. The architecture of Chandigarh
was dead, and up went the cartoons of a
dead sun, a stone man, a revolving lifeless hand spinning forlornly over the
shadows of Corb's belief that "the happy
town is the town that possesses an
architecture...."

Edward Stone went to India and made a
pleasant building, but architects
sneered: it was not heroic. Corbusian
polemics had taken architecture into a
bitter moral struggle which made merely
nice buildings look absurd. Only Mies,
in deference to his age, experience, and
undeniably impeccable taste, was allowed
to do pretty buildings. All others were
expected to join the ranks and engage in
some kind of holy war - whether it was
Wright's grass-roots religion of organic
architecture, Gropius's team for the
anonymous industrial crystal, or Corb's
battle cry to "draw up the human and

poetic plans of the new world. Let us
reconstruct everything: the roads, the
ports, the cities, the institutions...."
Of course, architects all over the world
loved it, because it gave their activities
the illusion of a new lease on cultural
relevance; it was thrilling to fantasize
that, as an architect, you sat at the
highest control board of the new world
game - higher even than the politicians
and social architects. ("Architecture
or revolution," sang Corb at the end of
his manifesto, "Revolution can be avoided.") And there were so many architects
now who were young and ambitious, and if
all the other artists - writers, musi-
cians, painters - could revolutionize
things, why couldn't they?

Back in World War II, Mme. Corb served tea
and brioches to the young architects-in-
uniform who liberated Paris and then went
around the corner to pay homage to the
man who proposed, in the Voisin Plan, to
tear down all the buildings that said to
people who went to Paris, This is Paris,
and later, heading for home, standing
with cinematic poise against the sky on

the decks of navy destroyers with wind
and surf and Dmitri Tiompkin crashing all
around them, they dreamed the American
press release dreams of the new world
beyond the horizon: shining towers set
down in a park that blossomed with peace
and joy to the distant hum of the clean
machines that made it all possible.

Soon the sound track ran out, but the
dreams were hard to forget, commissions
were small, isolated, or nonexistent,
the dreamer became a drawing board hack
just to meet the mortgage payments on
lesser dreams, and the summoned-up energy
turned to bitterness. By invoking their
hidden vanities, Corb made paranoia and
and artistic elitism the fashion for a
generation of architects, men who perhaps
weren't very gifted or who had bad luck,
who nevertheless attempted to live the
new spirit in purist white houses with
dried everlasting flowers in a blue glass
jug, with the Braun record player on the
wall-bracket bookshelf and the Olivetti
Lettera 22 on the desk, thousands of
architects who sat on Thonet chairs and
ate off TC-100 plates as selected for the

"Most of the
construction
that has
remade
the Chicago
skyline
has consisted
of hundreds of
high-rise
apartment
buildings
designed for the
comfort of
the upper
middle class
and the
enrichment
of real estate
developers,
contractors,
labor leaders,
and bankers,

who are
Daley's
principle
financial
backers at
campaign time.
Out of
his first
bond issue for
public works
Daley set
aside
seventeen
percent
for slum
clearance
in a city
that has some
of the
worst slums
in the
country.
During his
sixteen years
in office,
he has
torn down the
homes of
thirty
thousand
people
and put up
one-third as
many housing
units,
almost all
of them
priced far out
of the reach
of those
who were
displaced.
In his own
defense,

design collection of the Museum of Modern
Art and still couldn't get commissions
because they weren't related to the
Rockefellers, and who wanted all the
world to be aware of this injustice.
Corb: "The defeats of these last years
represent as many victories. Public
opinion, once aroused, will make itself
felt. Our own fate is similar to that of
comrades engaged in the same fight. Our
rejected plans will become public
accusers, and the day will come when
these same plans will force the officials
to change their attitudes...."

And all the architects shuffling around
in corduroy rallied to the easy participation mystique through which a lifetime
of nonachievement and unrealized ambition
became imbued with not only meaning but
pride. At a time when it was becoming
obvious that absolutely everybody is an
environmentalist, the Corb legacy exhorted
architects on to visions of greater and
greater design dictatorship, and when,
in the crunch of reality, it became clear
that such control was neither ethically
viable nor economically feasible in the

modern world, a generation of architects retreated into the existential closet of martyrdom for a lost cause. Ayn Rand's architect-hero blew up his compromised creation with leftover sticks of dynamite, and architecture, the noble art, bowed out in a tirade of polemical self-pitying prose.

The modern movement was an artistic movement, and it failed because the artists, the only people who could conceivably have gotten the thing off the ground, could not afford to build. The modern movement occurred when life-styles were being determined less by wealthy patrons operating out of palaces and more by artists who could not afford palaces, who could support the other arts because the other arts came in small, inexpensive packages, but architecture cost too much. So they put their creativity to use in the management of existing spaces, the usually very dreary spaces, which were all they could afford to rent, and very lucky they were indeed if they could find such a space to renew and re-create in the creative terms of its use. Factories,

44

warehouses, carriage houses, garrets,
coal barges, shanty backyard studios:
these were the workshops in which artists
tested the creative application of the
new sensibility of a polymorphous architecture, without the pretense of doing
anything architectural.

Internal walls were ripped out. In went
a macchinetta for making coffee, cushions
for sitting around on, straw matting
underneath the cushions, Navajo blankets
to insulate the walls, burlap to fix up
some closets, a table made out of a door,
orange crates to hold books, spot lamps
to light up canvases and make leafy shadows on the ceiling. In the hot summer
months tar dripped from the rafters, and
everybody went to the movies because they
were air-conditioned or out to the fire
escape to read, drink wine, or just take
long looks at the street.

Modern architecture had indeed arrived,
not in the form of buildings, which were
too big and cumbersome to be modern no
matter what shape they took, but in the
mothball bins of second-hand shops. The

...THAT REFORM
IS THE END
RESULT OF A
LIST OF THINGS
THAT "SHOULD"
OR "MUST" BE
DONE RATHER
THAN THE DOING
OF ANYTHING.

new style became truly international in
the sixties, when bands of poor charter-
jet gypsies took over islands and hotel
rooms and refurbished them with a patch-
work of denim, wall hangings, candles,
posters, incense, cassettes, and other
CARE package paraphernalia you could
carry in a bag or pick up near the site.

The fundamen-
tal bind:
the word
architecture,
implying the
existence of
the higher
meaning or
ideal,
naturally
lends itself
to programs
(such as
utopias)
doomed to
failure by the
importance
they give to
purely materi-
al and sensory
manipulations.

By ignoring the connections of luck and
labor that enabled some people to live
in fine places and forced others to spend
time in the slums, the modern movement
reduced its output to efficient shells
that had to be vacated every afternoon at
five to give everyone enough time to find
a real place to live by nightfall. The
modern movement came to the cities, and
everyone except blacks and artists fled
to the suburbs because in suburbia,
ironically, lay the greatest concentration
of sophisticated technology available at
the retail level for consumer space
conditioning and general take-home myth-
making, an unexpected cultural reversal
that shattered the conventional definition
of the city, created the megalopolis, and
left Jane Jacobs breathless.

The artists who stayed behind after the
great exodus of the fifties had to adopt
black life-styles (jazz, slang, drugs)
or perish, because a process of natural
urban selection had elected black people

"SPIRITUAL"
WORK
CUSTOMARILY
REGARDED AS
LUXURY
ONE CAN AFFORD
ONLY AFTER
ONE HAS
DESIGNED ONE-
SELF INTO
MATERIAL
AFFLUENCE.
WHICH THE CART?
WHICH THE
HORSE?
WHERE'S THE
CARROT?

the only group fit to live creatively
with the cumulative cultural disaster the
city had become. Since blacks had long
been acquainted with the delights of
"organic living" (for the reason that few
of them could afford appliances), they
were ideally suited to dominate an environment in which the technological cues
installed to remind one to be "civilized"
were constantly out of order. Blacks were
well aware that these breakdowns were to
their political advantage, as was demonstrated some years ago during the water
shortage in New York, when black leaders
urged Harlem residents to leave taps
running and flush their toilets as often
as possible.

The moral health of built America depended
upon a prevailing unwillingness to extend
political recognition beyond the perceptual patterns of the official (WASP) culture
which had designed it. The black contri-

47

bution to contemporary environments may
be measured by the degree to which blacks
were denied participation in creating the
old ones. They struggled to make a freedom for themselves within the structural
baffles of bulwarks they had no part in
shaping, within a brutalizing architecture
best symbolized by the prison cell. The
"friendly Negroes" Corb observed pushing
brooms through Grand Central inhabited
another world of rhythmic, invisible
structures which suddenly became visible
when the suburban exodus caused the
environmental franchise to be extended to
blacks by default.

This new vision, within the structure but
not part of it, recast the office towers
in the image of Babylon; redefined the
chic pink-lit hotel salons as padded cells
in the world's largest lunatic asylum, the
suburb as a mass and inadequate fallout
shelter full of electronic leaks, tools
whose artificial energy supply could be
cut off at any moment, leaving the color
Sunday supplement version of life high
and dry on the cultural junk heap. Black
architecture painted moustaches on white

buildings, used graffiti to warm uppity
monuments into dialogue with the people
compelled by circumstance to live among
them, used natural body energy to put
the tall office building, artistically
considered, to sexual shame.

In the twenties, when le jazz style was
exploding all over the world and
Josephine Baker was the rage of Paris,
when Mr. Fitzgerald and Miss Goober
Hudson and their friends were grabbing
limousines and heading uptown to the only
place in the West where anything vital
and spontaneous appeared to be going on -
the architect discovered the slum. To the
modern architect and other cryptoacademics
with cultural delusions of neoclassical
grandeur, it was an outrage that all this
creative energy could be happening outside
the mandarin mainstream. Corb went to
New York and witnessed the slums as
treacherous places that must be torn down
at once; then went back to Paris and
announced that he had returned the roof
to human use by making it flat and
installing dwarf trees, but up in
Harlem they'd been using the roof for

Homelessness,
hunger,
war:
the obvious
visual images
of evil.
All design
can do
is offer a
system for
erasing
the image,
"reforming"
the source of
evils
into newer,
more
contemporary
"forms."

years, on summer days and nights with
music, sex, and whatever else was needed
to turn one man's eyesore into the next
man's Xanadu.

Other artists working in smaller-scale
media were able to contain some of this
new energy by putting loud, jazzy colors
in a frame, or learning to play the right
riffs, or carrying a notebook around for
jotting down slang; but formal architecture had no such process of energy ex-
change. The energy could not be contained,
nor could it be ignored; hence the only
solution was to label it ugly, condemn it,
and tear it down. The destruction of the
ethnic cultural milieu, especially that
of the black, became the chief priority
of modern architecture under the title
Urban Renewal. "I don't see why our cities
can't be beautiful places, full of flowers
and pretty girls," sighed Ben Thompson,
head of Harvard's Graduate School of
Design, and everybody got behind the
campaign to stamp out the blight and sway
ethnic groups to the pursuit of tasteful,
gracious living. Countless renderings of
the renewed areas were mocked up, cartoons

Jung:
"The
fundamental
structure
of the
unconscious
is not
affected
by the
deviations
of our
ephemeral
consciousness."

50

of the new urban delight: yacht marinas
for the Harlem residents, peppermint-
striped umbrella stands vending Belgian
waffles on every corner of streets freshly
lined with strips of lift-off decal spider
trees. The races strolled arm in arm as
they made their afternoon purchases, down
a twinkle-light fairyland community arcade,
past a Parisian kiosk and a happy-go-lucky
balloon man; the children played with
hoops; and who could imagine that such a
pretty picture, bastard child of Camillo
Sitte and Marie Antoinette, could be
nothing but sheer insult?

*In contrast to
the space/time/
sociology/
salvation Grand
Design linkup:
a tradition of
works whose
idiosyncratic
vitality has
insured their
exclusion from
the standard
history of
architecture,
except in foot-
note references
(Pevsner gives
Gaudi one para-
graph) to their
irresponsible
deviations from
the mainstream
ethic of
professional
solidarity:*

If my treatment of the modern movement is
virulent, it is because it's hard to
respect the work of men who tried so hard
to establish themselves as the century's
prime cultural reactionaries. At a time
when other artists were demanding greater
freedom for all, the movement devoted its
energies to narrowing such freedom,
reducing expression to such pat authori-
tarian formulas as functionalism and grids.
The extension of architecture into town
and global planning led architects to
imagine that their solutions were correct

51

Soane's house, Fonthill Abbey, Bomarzo's monster garden, Jung's house, Wright's windmill, Cheval's chateau, Rodilla's Watts Towers, Kiesler's Endless House, Schmidt's tin-foil forest.... Works which do not parade them-selves as solu-tions beyond the fact of their having been made; which, by refus-ing to admit shame for their highly personal mode, are epiphanies of the best that illusion has to offer.

not for just a slice of the environment, but for the rest of the world as well. Corb would never have given Wright a permit to build his prairie house in the Radiant City, Wright would have barred Cartesian skyscrapers from Usonia, and the Miesian grid would have ruled out the possibility of either. And at a time when other arts were liberating themselves from the constraints of the academies, archi-tects were actually in the process of creating such institutions for themselves for the first time since the Middle Ages, in the form of professional organizations without whose official stamp one is legally prohibited from practicing architecture at all or even calling one's self an architect. This assured for architecture a stagnation not found in any other art, as Andy Warhol recognized when he remarked that architecture was "really the only thing left."

The hidden reactionism is expressed, too, in the process of doublespeak which uses philanthropic rhetoric to disguise the most blatant forms of social exploitation. Mies and Corb are great, but Robert Moses

If architecture
be nothing
but shadow play,
then
let the
architectural
work
be the shadow
of a single
graceful gesture
cast briefly
upon the
three-dimensional
screen of space
without
messianic
pretense,
a work as
spontaneously
created
as a hand
momentarily
suspended
between
candle and wall.
For
however long
they endure,
such a work
ceaselessly
communicates
the joy taken
in its making.
The
Grand Design,
which proposes
to freeze space
into a
grand universal
datum,
communicates
nothing
but
arrogance.

communicates. The U.S. student riots of
1968 originated from Columbia University,
where the strike began as a protest
against the university planners' exploitation of Harlem in preempting the community's main park as the site for a new
gymnasium. The offer to share the swimming
pool with local blacks was an empty
gesture, and the violent aftermath gave a
new twist to the meaning of Dr. Johnson's
dictum that "to build is to be robbed."
Architecture or revolution? Architecture
can be avoided. (But then where would we
get windows to smash?)

While the movement, back in the halcyon
days of the Bauhaus, toyed with the design
of shapes and the wording of jargon, two
contemporary quasi-Germans, Hitler and
Jung, were, in complementary ways,
creating architectural works of a strength
scarcely matched in modern times. This
strength springs from the fact that neither man recognized any academic separation
between works of space/architecture and
the energy of the people who used them.
They sought not to impose arbitrary
statements of visual aesthetics on men's

THE MODERN
ARCHITECT
MUST LIVE
WITH THE
CULTURAL
SUPPOSITION THAT
"THE SUREST TEST
OF THE
CIVILIZATION
OF A PEOPLE -
AT LEAST AS SURE
AS ANY -
AFFORDED BY
MECHANICAL ART
IS TO BE FOUND
IN THEIR
ARCHITECTURE,
WHICH PRESENTS
SO NOBLE A FIELD
FOR THE DISPLAY
OF THE GRAND,
THE BEAUTIFUL,
AND WHICH,
AT THE SAME TIME,
IS SO
INTIMATELY
CONNECTED
WITH THE
ESSENTIAL
COMFORTS OF
LIFE".
(WILLIAM
PRESCOTT,
THE CONQUEST
OF PERU)

eyes but to locate the means, if such a
means existed, by which human-inhabited
spaces became charged with an unconscious
power of cultural identity. Unlike the
designers, Hitler and Jung both knew that
architecture had to be cognizant of the
full range of cerebral and chthonic
experience if it hoped to engage the
system of psychic connections by which
the plastic environment is rendered by
human perceptions into place. Jung's
vision was cosmic, Hitler's mundane.

Hitler was much more than the frustrated
architect historians make him out to be;
he grasped the environmental tools that
modern architects could merely dream of.
Where Corb's Voisin Plan merely depicted
the buildings of Paris razed mainly as an
aesthetic statement, Hitler actually
wired the buildings with explosives.
Generated by an electronic darshan of
radio broadcasts and theatrically lit
political rallies, kept pure by education-
al programs and death camps, Hitler's
brief experiment was the only one-man
master plan of modern times to be realized
on a modern scale. Actual buildings were

...AND THIS IS
RATHER A
TERRIFIC
RESPONSIBILITY,
PARTICULARLY
AT A TIME WHEN
THE CONCEPT OF
COMFORT
IS SOMETHING
ONE WOULD RATHER
NOT EXPRESS
IN PUBLIC.

just props, of course - their design
delegated to journeymen like Speer.
Hitler's creation was Lebensraum, land
to breed dreams on, and the technological means with which to make them
credible.

Jung, meanwhile, was exploring the
avenues of self which led to a different
kind of living room, and over a period
of decades he built himself a house. His
work was the investigation of artifacts
in which the invisible essence of world
culture was made manifest, and the
modest tower in Bollingen incorporated
the fruit of his search in a hand-
fashioned personal-size system of
environmental fixes that transcend
academic ideas of art in serving the
twenty-four-hour-a-day continuum of
being on earth. Bollingen was not a
work of taste (which, as designers
understand the term, is simply blind
obedience to established patterns of
visual conditioning), but the crystalli-
zation of years of energy spent in the
psychic environment on a search for the
reason why. Each stone, its position and

carved inscriptions, gave meaning to the
life of the man who assembled them, used
symbolic language to connect that life
with the lives of other men. Compared to
Bollingen, Corb's houses appear as dated
and comically tacky as a thirties dress;
Mies's pavilions look as inviting as a
Greyhound waiting room; Wright's prairie
houses are revealed as a naive attempt to
market the visual trappings of domestic
security to buyers for whom such values
lacked the substance of individual
achievement. Jung's control of environment is justified by the acts of perpetual use in which the self remains master
over the spaces, times, and eclectic
cultural references of which Jung himself was the vital connecting center.

Hitler's "folkish" architecture and
Jung's psychological perception both
groped for the keys to meaning in the
use of space, but whereas Hitler's vision
was limited by the fact that those on
whom it was imposed could never comprehend it fully from within, Jung's
achievement, a building built to serve
the builder exclusively, used the act of

making structure as an integral part of the process of psychic development. As an experiment in restoring to man a tangible diagram of his inner growth, the Bollingen tower is uniquely successful in the history of modern building. The tower rejects the role of architect; it rejects the assumption that a man can meaningfully modify the living space of another; it rejects the importance attached to modern materials and methods and modern concepts of usefulness; it rejects the beauty parlor styling of spaces that delights the static eye and ignores the other senses and processes by which the wide range of affinities, experiences, and communication systems achieves the symbiosis of individual and group reality.

As such, it exemplifies a process which everybody follows. The cultural fabric need not be self-consciously created as a harmonic entity, and everyone is free to walk among the piles of artifacts and select from them the material to shape an environmental structure. It is precisely this freedom that is lacking in the work of artists who follow Corb in presuming

Lincoln Center, Kennedy Center: symbols of a Ptolemaic era of the West; vital forms copied into lifeless renditions; supported for the benefit of show, political popularity, and because they are the well-tried forms everyone knows. New York as Alexandria.

HOW
GLASS
ARCHITECTURE
WAS
ORIGINALLY
CONCEIVED BY
THE
GERMAN GLASS
FANATICS
(INSPIRED BY
SCHEERBART)
AS A MEANS
OF SHATTERING
CONVENTIONAL
BOURGEOIS
DOMESTIC
STANDARDS,
AND HOW
GLASS
ARCHITECTURE
HAS WOUND UP
BEING
EXCLUSIVELY
THE
ENVIRONMENT
OF THE
MOST
THOROUGHLY
BOURGEOIS
AND
MATERIALISTIC
ELEMENTS IN
MODERN
SOCIETY -
A
TRANSMOGRIFI-
CATION.

that "as an architect I may say that
architecture is an event in itself. It
can live entirely upon itself..." without
the identity imparted to it by the
creative processes of use, whether pri-
vately, as in Jung's case, or by the
group. The architectural obsession with
white walls, clean surfaces, and naked
lighting fixtures reflects a neurotic
refusal to accept the fundamental organic
systems in which beings, space, and time
achieve a satisfying environmental
metabolism. All spaces are servant
spaces, or else they are dead. The
environmental integrity found at
Bollingen, which is lacking in most
contemporary buildings, stems from precisely this knowledge.

Jung was afraid to go to Rome. He tried.
He got as far as Pompeii before he
backed out. He feared the master pull of
such an intense concentration of mundane
energy, the dense layering of secular
rituals that had shaped the culture from
whose last decadent gasp he worked his
whole life to escape. The air in Rome
was poisoned, especially at night when

the ghosts of history fluttered down
like antique costumes, preventing the
modern age from discovering itself.

Pitched halfway on the space/time scale
between civilization and the Universal
City, New York City has no such restraints
on its virility, and there the morality
of poison passes from the mundane to the
hysterically sublime. Ugliness, fatigue,
drama, boredom, danger, noise, and
hopelessness combine in quantity sufficient to mesmerize, transmogrifying
random quirks and flashes into the
mercurial gestalt of the holy city, the
place where the simple act of being is
enough to sustain the progress of the
hours. Nothing is believed, no one is
saved. The dogshit dialogue, the many
city forms of grit, the grace of garbage,
and the innocent squalor of ragbag mis-
takes take one ironically closer to Eden
than all the attempts at beauty control,
the drawing board versions of paradise,
could ever manage to do. The glass of curtain walls and shop windows reflects
dimensions that cannot be duplicated by
men except in the insect life spans of

SKYSCRAPERS,
HIGHWAYS (UNLIKE
PALACES, VILLAGES)
NONDUPLICABLE IN
THE MOVIE STUDIO
- WHY FILMING
MUST MOVE ON
LOCATION TO
CAPTURE THE
MODERN PLACE,
THUS COMPLETELY
ALTERING A
NATION'S
ENVIRONMENTAL
SENSIBILITIES.   59

fashion. The highest ideals of humanity are assumed with unparalleled relish, instantly digested, and thrown out with the trash. In the dormitory of danger, there is no fear of death.

One lives there and beholds no architecture; all is perenially plastic, intuitive, sacred beyond the sum of its secular parts. It was very trendy of Venturi to take his Yale design class to Las Vegas for a semester, but Las Vegas is an X ray of very old-fashioned architecture, merely enlarged in neon. In New York the ether is so dense you can't even see the electric signs, much less the buildings behind them. It is always a shock to notice, as one does on rare, split-second occasions, that New York has buildings, and that the buildings there are just like buildings anywhere else, no different from buildings in the great waste stretches of small midwestern cities. For example: the same old street-row architecture, the same standard details around windows and doorway, arbitrarily varied from block to block,

"Magically inscribed" facing-stone removed from the Great Pyramid to provide materials for "insignificant buildings" in Cairo, etc. But Herodotus says that these magical inscriptions were merely lists comparable in banality to the pop art poetry of Linear B, recording such profound cosmic truths as the quantities of garlic and onions consumed by the workmen during the course of construction

60

- a vernacular
beyond
Venturi's
wildest dreams.
(Imagine
United Nations
headquarters
inscribed with
the number of
cups of coffee,
bologna
sandwiches,
doughnuts)....

from building to building. Usually your
eyes bear witness to nothing architectural; building after building, all
blending into a rising and setting miasma;
the reality of a figurative climax at
every red light; the flurry of a million
separate moving parts hitting, missing,
hitting, and running, generating the
white-heat conditions that make a mirage.

New York is the world's most medieval
city: the narrow streets, buildings
meeting at the top, squalor, paranoid
nightwalkers, the skill required to steer
yourself around the Scylla and Charybdis
on every block, a whole life of drowning
flashbacks encountered on every corner
waiting for the light to change. Heading
uptown or downtown in a cab, falling
apart, lighting cigarettes, humming songs
in a traffic jam, laughing at the amaze-
ment of always being two or three hours
late, and in the midst of it you are
always there, in New York, pretending not
to wait, and sometimes X and Y get together
and you just have to celebrate the fact
that there's no design like the present.

IN UNIVERSE
OF RELATIVITY,
ONLY ONE STANDARD
IN ART:
IS IT INTERESTING
OR IS IT CORNY?
(THIS THROWS IT
ALL BACK
ON THE OBSERVER,
HIS
RELATIVE DEGREE
OF EXPERIENCE.)
ALL OTHER
STANDARDS
(LIGHT AND SHADOW,
COMPOSITION,
RHYTHM,
BALANCE,
CONSISTENCY OF
STYLE, ETC.)
DEPEND ON
BELIEF IN
PERCEPTUAL
ABSOLUTES
NOT OPERATING
IN THIS
UNIVERSE.

Far from the semitropical drumbeat island where you alone possess all the
energy you need to shape the day's
events, this is a place where there are
so many psychic covers placed layer upon
layer between you and the planets that
you have to buy houseloads of extra
energy from Con Ed to forge the simple
connections necessary to personal sanity.
The Pan Am building provides a perpetual
full-moon logo over Manhattan's lunar
frenzy; the towers at night form a
gigantic planetarium showing forth the
flourescent constellations of the
New York process. People have gathered
together here to turn out weekly editions of the catalog of software
essential to the process of filling up
time. That this appears to some to be a
fundamentally immoral practice is irrelevant. Those who think that the
emperor has no clothes are unfit for
their station and go off to become
critics.

For in New York one learns that environments are epiphanies of human nature; one
passes judgment on them at the risk of

62

City streets
at night,
haunted,
bleary, -
closed shops.
Fodder
for the new
architectural
Process designs
- for "24-Hour
City" and such.
But
they are so
completed
and beautiful
at night.
They
remain open
all night
as streets
full of
closed shops,
expressing
their openness
by being closed;
it is
the other side
of their life.
The
architectural
mind
finds such change
and variety
extremely odious.
(Corb's proposal
to air-condition
all buildings
to the same
exact
temperature;
Fuller's
domed cities.)

exposing one's failure to use them to
advantage. Environments are practical
jokes played on space - when the joke
begins to backfire, it's time to begin
again. The demolition of buildings, an
activity of paramount importance to the
working strength of New York, is highly
valuable in providing visual evidence of
the mortality of the environmental con-
ventions we often take for granted. Here
one day and gone the next, environments
are shaped by perceptual patterns determined by the character of our motivations. As motivations change so does
perception, and thus "the environment"
is altered.

There is nothing at all new about environmental pollution apart from the fact
that only recently have cultural motivations combined to create the formula by
which pollution is perceived as an
enriching aspect of conditioned space.
Space contains both litter and litter
basket. Culture created the town and the
outskirts of town, and then obliterated
the barriers as populations grew. Culture
defines the awareness of room in terms of

63

a room or several rooms and is free to
shatter that convention whenever necessary. Space abides over the eternal process of its use, whether for just or
unjust, moral or immoral purposes. None
of them last. There are no implications
for design.

Although the act of building for others
is more a manifestation of an individual's ego power than the expression of a
common cultural language (except insofar
as such languages are themselves the
cumulative creations, in part, of ego
power), it comes as no surprise that in
the age of democracy and the welfare
state, architects, who often rely on
modesty as the ultimate form of conceit,
should be earnest in attempting to
dedicate their services to the mythical
commonweal. Perhaps it is in just this
connection - in the assumption that some
can provide others with the stuff of
better living - that contemporary architecture falls furthest from the mark in
assessing the truths and potentials of
environment.

The history of utopia-designing is an
account of the struggle to attain goals
within the "earthbound confines of the
physical plane," a parable of the fruit-
lessness of trying to harness material
tools to "enlightened" thinking. The
utopia tradition began with the early
industrial mentality of eighteenth-
century Europe, the period when architecture began to lose its grip on environmental control. In a cultural setting
in which the divine right of kings was
still a potent belief, it was possible
to contemplate the future as a series of
well-ordered changes, directed from
above for the benefit of all.

French philosophers such as Fournier
began advancing the idea that all human
ills were caused by defects in the human
environment and proceeded to outline
plans for future-changes in a series of
logical, well-intended theories whereby
all men might share the burden of ar-
rested development reflected unwittingly
by their own naive thinking. Fournier
envisioned the whole globe willingly

No need
to wait around
for Safdie's
proposed
house-producing
machine;
everyone already
has one,
every
environment
custom-made to
perception.

"After
the red wine
we set out
to look for
a studio.
Raymond knew
two words
of French
and we walked
along the
streets
saying
"Chercher
atelier."
What we did not
know was that
atelier does not
mean a studio
in France,
but any kind of
workshop.
Finally,
at dusk
we found a
studio in a
courtyard,
at the extraor-
dinary price of
fifty francs
a month,
furnished.
We were
overjoyed,
and paid a
month in advance.
We could not
imagine why it
was so cheap,
but that night
we found out.

regrouped into an international confed-
eration of "phalanxes" with its capital
at Constantinople. Each phalanx, a
parallelogram in plan, would consist of
precisely 1,500 people engaged in useful
production exactly divided between
agriculture and industry. All sense of
practicality was surrendered to the need
of the rational mind to exclude that
which could not be ordered in terms of
an ideal symmetry. Jobs would be determined by what a person was considered
"best fitted for." Example: since
children, as is well known to be universally true, love to play with dirt,
they would naturally be elected the
community garbage collectors.

In the 1820s the British industrialist
Robert Owen purchased 30,000 acres of
land in America, on the banks of the
Wabash, and began setting up the city of
New Harmony, a community "woven out of
the powerful yarn of interest and the
silken thread of love...planned with
careful attention to the most important
discoveries in science, as to form a new
combination of circumstances capable of

Just as we had composed ourselves to rest, terrific earthquakes seemed to shake the studio and the whole thing seemed to jump into the air and then fall flat. This was repeated over and over again. Raymond went down to inspect, and found that we were refuged over a night imprimerie. Hence the cheapness of the studio. It somewhat dampened our spirits but, as fifty francs meant a great deal to us in those days, I proposed that it sounded like the sea and that we should pretend we were at the seaside."
—Isadora Duncan, My Life

producing permanently greater physical, moral and intellectual advantages to every individual than have ever been realized in any age or country." While New Harmony is aesthetically significant as one of the first designs for the modern architectural megastructure (a single building containing all living, working, and leisure spaces), the experiment itself was a failure. They built a few shacks, about 800 freeloaders showed up for dinner, the project ran into enormous debt, and Owen, frustrated, sold the land after five years and returned to England to create genuine social change on the levels where change was possible: reform of government, education, and blue-collar working conditions.

Far from profiting from Owen's lesson in the politics of environments, architects over the past century and a half have made the design of utopias the master-piece assignment in qualifying for architectural fame - inspired by an equal mixture of sound intentions and the frustration of being unable to secure "important" commissions. These projects

67

confirm the consistency with which architects refuse to work with the materials
and methods which, in any given cultural
situation, are the viable agents for the
changes they seek to accomplish.

In the sooty, upholstered environment of
early Victorian England, Pugin convinced
fellow architects that by erecting all
buildings in the true Gothic style they
could return society to the pious model
of the Middle Ages. In Catholic France
a hundred years later, on the other hand,
Tony Garnier's proposed cité industrielle
contained no churches. In lazy, sunny
Italy, Sant'Elia saw the coming utopia as
a clockwork community of highly efficient airport personnel. Bruno Taut's
Alpine fantasies conjured up cosmic
visions of colorfully robed throngs in a
pantheistic procession up mountain paths
lined with silver columns, to the music
produced by gusts of wind blowing through
colossal glass pipes - a bizarre solution
to the environmental needs of a "nation
of watchmakers."

The repetitive boredom of Corb's Radiant
City was seen at its best from an endless

Dear Abby:
My neighbor's windchimes are driving me batty! I listened to those chimes all last summer and if I have to listen to them again this summer I'll go mad, but what can I do? This neighbor has hung the chimes on a tree which is right outside my bedroom window. She has air conditioning and I don't, so I have to raise my window when I retire and all I can hear is tinkling and clinging and clanging until I could just about jump out of my skin! Of what earthly good are those chimes anyway? I have a good relationship with this neighbor, who is very nice, and I don't want her to get angry with me, so please help me solve this problem peacefully.

GOING BATTY

ideal terrace cafe floating in the air. Wright designed special cars to transport the new Usonians through the square-off suburban monotony of his Broadacre City, uninspired at any speed. According to the Ekistics Creed of Doxiadis, the utopia was not merely aesthetically desirable but was a social necessity to insure the survival of civilization. From his studio outside the Motor City, Eliel Saarinen issued plans for the modern city based upon microphotographic blowups of the cell structure of leaves. Fuller's Dymaxion world took up the neo-white man's burden, shoving the apotheosis of the American good life as U.S. grant "design science" research down the throats of unenfranchised populations reduced to computer statistics. Next come Paolo Soleri's cosmic-comical pueblo arcologies, followed by the hovercraft jokemobiles of Archigram's plug-in city, tossing out leaflets of a camp sophistication as they hover down the streets of working-class districts in Birmingham and Manchester. The apparently wide variety among these solutions is confined to superficial graphic trappings. In fact all these projects, works that

...*a universe*
in which
Mr. and Mrs. Doe
may regard
as a Communist
conspiracy
the extraction
from their bodies
of a
postprandial fart
to help maintain
the
gaseous balance
of the
local biosphere...
of
interrelatedness
which
architecture and
other synthetic
languages
conspire to
conceal.

crown the careers of their creators, that
are taken to represent the highest
developments in architectural thought,
are identical. They are alike, to begin
with, in their inappropriateness to the
situations they purport to solve, but
more important is their similarity in
perpetuating the same tired illusion that
the act of building is an act which
affects the quality of human life.

There is, of course, the argument that
if you replace a decrepit school, one in
which the rats in the baseboard distract
students' attention, with a newer school,
the quality of education may change.
Whether this is valid or not is beside the
point. The schoolhouse argument addresses
its attention to specifics; the utopia
tradition does not. The utopia tradition
encourages the design of buildings not
for people at all but for the ideal
graphic symbols of men and women that
wander like happy lobotomy victims
through renderings of worlds in which a
rat never set foot.

The issue would not be worth bothering
about if the utopian architect regarded

his work as an environmental folly along
the lines of Bomarzo and Fonthill Abbey,
a building designed for ghosts like
Sarah Winchester's place, or as something
no more capable of being built than
Escher's Belvedere, but this is not the
case. Instead, he asks his project to be
regarded as the "real" solution, a
realizable key to a permanent social
salvation - doubtless designed with very
careful attention to the discoveries of
modern science, but way off the track in
the assumption that such facts, figures,
and accordingly well-laid plans are of
much importance in the process by which
men use space to achieve what utopia-
designers themselves identify as the
objective of their work: meaning, joy,
satisfaction, liberation, peace, happi-
ness, wisdom, or whatever.

Fuller's 200-foot Geoscope is the
sovereign orb of the new academic
imperialism. Fuller claims that earlier
utopian attempts failed because they
tried to alter men rather than the
environment, but the philosophes were as
utterly convinced as he is that the
defects lay in the latter. Fuller's

71

In many
unincorporated
Florida
communities
there are
no public
services such as
garbage
collection and
fire department,
and you must
maintain
a perfect green
grass lawn
(which is very
difficult and
expensive to do,
since of course
grass doesn't
grown there
naturally),
or you will be
thrown out
of the community
residents'
organization,
in which case
no one
will collect your
garbage,
and if
your house
should catch
on fire
no one will come
to put it out.

dictum "Reform the environment - not man"
springs directly from Fournier and
reveals the essentially atavistic appeal
of the Dymaxion vision. For those unac-
quainted with the history of utopia
(apart from the Fuller version), or for
those who think that Malthus is still
hot stuff, the vision is no doubt exciting. Fuller has discovered that technology has reached the point where it can
make the old pretechnology dreams come
true at last. It is a persistently annoy-
ing habit of old dreams to come true long
after they have ceased to be vital, which
is why such changes, when they occur, are
always transmogrifications rather than
transformations. Dreams are cheap, and
they come true in meretricious form.
Everybody has a college degree and is
perplexed that no one is impressed. There
is a chicken in every pot, but it is
frozen, shot full of carcinogenic hor-
mones, and tasteless. Everybody has a
suburban villa and finds it a depressing
place to come home to. Everybody has a
work station carefully designed for maxi-
mum efficiency and soon is restless

because there is no more vital work to be
done in a stationary position, except by
computers. Even when everybody has been
placed in Fuller tetrahedral ghettos of
force-fed abundance, we will have yet to
teach ourselves how to endure the appal-
ling banality without niacin or other
kinds of acid. The irony is that Fuller's
missionaries are drawn exclusively from
the middle-class, academic prototypes of
these ghettos already in successful
operation; they are buying their way out
at the expense of those they manage to
tempt into the .01 percent nightmare of
success. Is there life after design?

...ENERGY
TO CARRY
BUILDINGS AND
WORDS
FROM THE
FOUNDATIONS
TO THE
FANTASIES.

Now into one of those aimless whirligigs
where the old cultural tradition of high
abstract ideals tugs against clumsy
formulas for daily survival: Is the purpose of architecture to give architects
something to do with their time on earth
and the income to live well and raise a
family, or is there some higher purpose?
If no higher purpose, must one be
invented? If so, who gets to invent it?
One architect? A group of architects

working together under a group name? An
international convention of architects?
Architectural journalists? Scientists?
Politicians? Existentialists? And would
the invention of a higher purpose produce
the slightest effect on architecture?

Assurance for those troubled with such
academic questions comes from all quar-
ters, and in retrospect it becomes clear
that, for at least the past century and
a half, the single most important function of architecture has been to find a
function for architecture in a world
that has lost the ground of common
ideological purpose which, long ago,
charged buildings with the ritual energy
of events.

When architecture goes beyond the simple
task of providing shelter from the storm,
the direction it may take is any man's
guess. When imagination fails, one can
always fall back on the academic deca-
dence of formalized aesthetics, the
thing-of-beauty-is-a-joy-forever syndrome,
as Vitruvius did when he eulogized the
Greeks, as Philip Johnson does when he

'Search
for the
perfect chair:
relevant only
in a universe
in which
rest is the norm,
in which
the act of
sitting
is considered
"natural,"
or in which
certain postures
are deemed
universal.
Every table,
chair,
ashtray
is perfect
for what it is
perfect for,
if not for
sitting
then for making
chairs.
Western idea
of chair
derived from
Egyptian throne
which was
never intended
for sitting,
anyway.

says that the purpose of architecture is
to satisfy the need for beautiful buildings - the need, in other words, for
tasteful surroundings. But the rules of
good taste are not absolutes, obviously,
and what is no doubt the right attitude
to have when shopping for curtains and
carpets for the den passes into unaccept-
able presumptuousness as one moves into
the public domain in which the key monuments of architecture have heretofore
been located. Philip Johnson would have
been a great architect had he given up
building after building his own house.

Just a few decades ago, the Italian
futurists pointed out the beauty of cars
and planes, but now we fix our eyes on
the exhaust fumes and are less enraptured.
As the work of many artists recently has
been to demonstrate the perceptual apparatus by which the beauty in absolutely
everything may be appreciated, it seems a
rather redundant gesture for an artist to
cling to the static beauty quotients (the
golden mean, the inherent beauty of
materials, the logical use of ornament,
and so on) as the guidelines of his work.

The question of the stylishness of Mies and Johnson's Seagram Building versus the crassness of Skidmore's Lever House is immaterial in light of the fact that neither is designed to last more than forty years. Why all the travertine fuss?

The architect's role has carried great cultural prestige for centuries. Western civilization created God in the image of an anthropomorphic architect, and from this it followed reasonably that architects should try to style themselves as gods on earth. Sooner or later the illusion was bound to crumble, depositing the architect on the level of cultural meaning occupied by others whose business is conditioning space: firemen, garbage collectors, window dressers, cops - all of us who wear bright or faded colors in the street, flush the toilet, make the bed.

If the design of utopias is the artistic response to the increasing inability of buildings to shape events, then the science of archaeology is the utopia's cultural counterpart. The two traditions

AS OUR CULTURE
IS POPULARLY
CONSTITUTED,
PEOPLE PROBABLY
"WEREN'T MEANT
TO" LIVE IN
ENVIRONMENTS
OF CONSTANT
TEMPERATUTE
(CENTRAL HEAT,
AIR CONDITION-
ING, ETC.).
BUT OF COURSE
THEY WILL
ANYWAY,
AND NATURALLY
THE CULTURAL
CONSTITUTION
WILL BE
AMENDED
IN DUE COURSE.

76

THIS IN ITSELF
IS NOT
INTERESTING,
BUT WHAT IS
WHEN YOU FIND
THESE PEOPLE
BALKING
AT THE NOTION
OF CHANGES
THAT THEY
THEMSELVES HAVE
PRECIPITATED,
PRECISELY
THROUGH SUCH
THINGS AS
CENTRAL HEATING,
TWO CARS, ETC.

sprang up at the same time and place
(mid-eighteenth-century Europe) to
mutually reinforce the escapist mentality
which most people needed to cushion the
shock of living in a period of such rapid
change. Together with other forms of
fiction, they managed to postpone this
shock for two centuries, until pedestrian
perceptions (Alvin Toffler's, for example)
were able to contain it without undue
nervous stress, by which time the period
of transition was over; rapid change had
become the norm.

The archaeologist donned the mantle of
rational scientific research, went off in
search of Eden, Troy, Atlantis, Avalon,
and other mythical paradises, and came
back to the present with stones from the
past, relics that served as exhibits to
strengthen the designer's vision of the
future. "And did those feet in ancient
times...?" was the preface to the port-
folio of plans for the New Jerusalem,
for deliverance from the "dark, satanic
mills" of the Industrial Revolution, from
the reality, in other words, which made
architecture, as it was understood, as

77

Invention of technopak sensory aid, similar to hearing aid and eyeglasses, to correct the kinesthetic sense to some perceptual norm. Movies, TV, etc., have stimulated this sense, albeit rather crudely; further research needed to produce a device that does what TV does, but without the burden imposed by visual program material. An instrument equivalent to the light bulb, transmitting pure kinetic energy as the bulb transmits pure visual energy.

obsolete as the horse-drawn charrette. Architects designed ready-made ruins, set them down in carefully engineered "natural settings" - symbols of the new Arcadia.

Early archaeologists concentrated on the piles of classical antiquity which, while romantically distant, yet belonged to the "continuous evolutionary curve of historical architecture" later traced out by Fletcher. But as the plain facts about these cultures came rolling in to be tagged in increasing numbers, romance waned. The breakthrough in deciphering Linear B did not reveal philosophical insights or works of an inspired poetic beauty but rather a collection of shopping and laundry lists. Recently, therefore, the vogue has shifted to works built before there was a history to betray their true cultural context: Stonehenge, Avebury, Silbury Hill, the Great Pyramid, the Great Wall of China - these are the signposts along the newest environmental escape routes. By creating a past as vague as the future, these structures serve as the vapor screen on which the

designer projects the higher cultural
purpose he is unable to detect in the
present environment, the image of the
grail that makes his work seem more than
Pollyanna babblings. It is no surprise
to find Buckminster Fuller lending in-
formal encouragement to speculative
analysis of the prehistoric system of
spatial configurations at Glastonbury,
for Fuller's utopian view finds the same
completion in John Michell's View Over
Atlantis that eighteenth-century
antiquarian architects drew from books
like Wood's Ruins of Baalbec.

The new occult-archaeological interpretations, while fascinating in themselves,
limit understanding of the ancient
structures by arbitrarily introducing an
artificial separation of some kind
(usually a natural catastophe) between
our world and the world that produced
them, after the manner of the earliest
archaeologists who divided the history
of architecture into two groups: Christian and pagan. If we surrender the
conditioning of this kind of past/future
chauvinism and follow the premise that

ACCIDENTS
CAUSED ON
FRENCH COUNTRY
ROADS
BY ALPHA RHYTHMS
CREATED BY
THE SUN
PERCEIVED AT
CERTAIN CAR
SPEEDS,
SHINING THROUGH
REGULARLY
PLANTED POPLARS.

the most fundamental human motivations
have changed little during the time men
have been making architecture, if we
define the history of architecture broad-
ly as the monograph of different ways in
which these motivations are spatially
resolved over the scale of time (rather
than limit it to an evolutionary curve of
construction techniques and visual aesthetics), the barrier dissolves and the
achievement of the ancient builders becomes clear.

VILLAGE OF
AVEBURY GROWING
UP IN THE CENTER
OF A PREHISTORIC
CIRCULAR
CONFIGURATION
WHOSE PRESENCE
WAS NOT EVEN
SUSPECTED UNTIL
A TRAVELER RIDING
THROUGH ON
HORSEBACK
SUDDENLY PER-
CEIVED IT...
KINESTHETIC
EXPERIENCE
BREEDING GREATER
AWARENESS OF
ANCIENT, EQUALLY
UNFRAGMENTED
ENVIRONMENTAL
SYSTEMS.

There is only one architectural style,
and from caves to space capsules there
has never been more than one: the universal style. Textbook "styles" are just
variations and components of the universal
style, mere reflections of the universal
process by which men in different places
and different times interpret the same
phenomena differently. Buildings have
different styles, but architecture has
only one because it has but one function:
to engage men in the process by which
their individual and collective energy is
brought into harmony with diagrams that
are taken to reflect absolute and univer-

sal patterns. This is as true of Route 66
as it is of England's prehistoric system
of ley-lines, as valid for Orly airport
as for the monuments on Easter Island.
Value judgments as to which is "better,"
"more human," "more natural," "more highly
evolved," "more deeply spiritual," etc.
are predicted upon the examination of
selected artifacts at the expense of ignoring the culture as an integrated
whole, which is why Rudofsky's superb
Architecture Without Architects has no
design implications apart from its already widespread use as coffee table
decor.

There is nothing mythical about the universal style. It is no more than the
architectural projection of the desire to
create meaning on all levels of experience - secular, holy, down to the most
trivial. It is the environmental expression of the mechanism that causes men to
form opinions and beliefs, to hold views
and convictions, and to propagate these
views - about whether the world is round
or flat, whether or not God exists (if so
what He looks like), which is the best

81

Not a word
in this book
about those
nifty Italian
plastic designs,
but in 1968
I was the person
at Design
Research
who had to dust,
clean,
arrange,
accessorize,
and light
those carefree
items,
patch those
blowup chairs,
make the
Joe Colombo
chairs
look as though
they belonged
somewhere other
than in an
operating room,
render the whole
collection
into something
faintly,
yet accessibly,
space-age;
and it was
one hell of
a challenge to
one's ingenuity,

as the
natural tendency
of these pieces
two days out
of the wrappings
was to go
the dismal,
scratched-up way
of all
modern campus
low-maintenance
vinyl
student lounges
everywhere.
Anyway Il Designo
never seemed
new to me;
I think it's to
Bauhaus design
what rococo
was to
baroque -
a fanciful
collection of
eye-catching
dust catchers.
Despite the
sensuous curves,
the cute
hardware details,
the bright
candy colors,
Il Designo
just carries on
the Bauhous
tradition of
perversely
trying to harness
industrial
techniques
to an elite
sensibility
while proclaim-
ing good taste
for the masses.

brand of Scotch, which colors go well together, what the role of government
should be. It is the Platonic search for
the perfect table, that state of conditioned mind that makes New Yorkers in-
credulous that anyone could be genuinely
happy outside New York, that makes Third
World backpacking travelers deny the possibility of life in any city, that insists
that the sun never sets on England. It is
the pride in wearing labels, the search
for the universal language predicted in
the Book of Revelations (D.W. Griffith
was convinced it was the movies), the
process which projects personal taste into
philosophic absolutes, which argues,
which presents proof, which believes that
all questions are made to be answered. It
is the mechanism used to find one's self
reflected in other people and situations
outside one's self, the invention of so-
called universal patterns, and the media
used to make others aware of these patterns. It is the attempt to "find one's
self" with relation to the universe, to
integrate into a whole meaningful pattern
the experience which one has had to break

82

down into separate little parts in order
to communicate this experience to others.

Men were able to make civilizations by
perfecting techniques that let them contain all the information they needed to
communicate to each other, and also let
them screen out (sour-grapes style) the
information that could not be so nicely
packaged. Architecture is such a technique. Architecture provides shelter not
just from rain and cold but from all and
everything. Architecture prevents the
oceanic floods of total information from
rushing in and brutalizing the senses
into sensory paralysis, thus destroying
the individual's illusion of his individ-
uality, the civilization's illusion of
its unique correctness. The architectural
experience is that of Narcissus disguised
as Prometheus. Tourists taking turns
around the observation platform of the
Empire State Building pause to reflect
that, yes, we are, after all, better than
just animals. Architecture provides
screens against the possible as well as
arenas of the pseudoabsolute; architec-

Presumably
the masses
with servants,
or the masses
who have nothing
to do but
sit around and
polish plastic
all day long.
I admit to using
Ettore Sotsass's
bright red
plastic
Olivetti
typewriter,
but after three
years of
never cleaning
it and
forgetting to
put it back in
its case except
when I travel
(when it never
fails to elicit
the greatest
interest
from the
hijack search
squad),
it's become
wonderfully
organic looking,
quite covered
with hair like
that famous
surrealistic
teacup.

ture tells people who need to be told
what to do, what to do. Successful architecture says it in such a way that
nobody notices that the barriers to uncon-
ditional experience are in themselves perceived as access routes to potential
freedom.

To the ancient Chinese, freedom followed
obedience to the "Way," and the architectural application of Taoism was to culti-
vate the garden, to transform all terri-
tory into a yin-yang landscape which
achieved perfect balance through the
faculty of the senses. Wind chimes and
kites (not just ornamental devices, but
sophisticated energy counters designed to
render the invisible into a sensory manifestation) were equally important as
buildings in setting up this universal
diagram. Because the setting-up process
did not involve a super high-level mechanical technology, it is a very appealing
model just now to Western whole-earth
environmental escape artists, just as the
Japanese six-by twelve-foot mat module
was celebrated by international style designers. It seems very high, very pure.

GRAND HOTEL
CONCEPT
OF PLUSH
IS REPLACED BY
SPACESHIP EARTH
AS NEWEST
TASTE FANTASY,
EVERYBODY'S
FAVORITE
ENVIRONMENTAL
FICTION.
IN THRILLING
CITIES
LIKE NEW YORK,
MANY PEOPLE,
RICH AND WELL-
EDUCATED,
LEAD INCREDIBLY
HUMDRUM LIVES;
AND OUT
THEY GO
ON SATURDAYS
TO PLACE THE
NEW SPACE AGE
INTELLECTUAL,
BUYING THAT
PLASTIC LAMP
OR THIS
BLOWUP CHAIR
AND FEELING,
IF ONLY ON
SATURDAYS,
THAT THEY'RE
PARTICIPATING.

But in fact the Chinese vision was just
as synthetic, as artificially imposed,
required just as much arbitrary conditioning, as the Western steam-shovel
transformations, being the expression of
an inflexible "inhuman" social system
with so little sign of change until Mao's
cultural revolution; a system which, if
it was free from Western neurotic symp-
toms, certainly had enough of its own
(such as koro, the Oriental male's paranoid fear of shrinking genitalia). History is already laughing up its sleeve
at the material prostitution of Eastern
ideas by the West, the art of kidnapping
empty forms of which Wright was an early
master. The temple wind chimes that provide one man with cosmic inspiration are
the source of his neighbor's insomnia.

The West has its own symbols. The car and
the airplane are symbols of spatial freedom for contemporary America. They take
you nowhere but are built in the image
of instruments designed to carry you
anywhere your heart desires. Airports
are exhilarating places for this reason;
they are concrete symbols of man's free

BEN THOMPSON OF
DESIGN RESEARCH:
"WE SIMPLY DON'T
RECOGNIZE
FASHION."

Rudofsky:
"Venacular
architecture
does not go
through
fashion cycles.
It is nearly
immutable,
indeed
unimprovable,
since it
serves its
purpose to
perfection.

will. Both Eastern and Western techniques
do nothing more than prescribe a program of environmental fixes to support
the human habit-at; define a place on
earth for men who might not otherwise
feel at home.

There were techniques before architecture
that had precisely the same function. If
architecture is often considered the
earliest, it is because architecture was
produced by the same universal system
which also hit on the idea of history to
record men's activities. Speculation on
the nature of the earlier software systems is the priority of anthropologists
who say that the earliest human habitats
were probably olfactory environments,
conditioned by the ability to perceive
smell. The earliest walls or barriers were
therefore synthesized in the part of the
brain that differentiates the sensation
of some smells from that of others, just
as, in the later visual universe, the
visual center was employed in construct-
ing walls to separate some spaces from
other spaces. But while the olfactory
universe may have been adequate for men

86

*Always,
always,
this contempt
for fashion.
An English
architecture
magazine,
internationally
famous as the
most forward-
thinking of
such journals,
asked me not
to show them
any more
of my writing
after I
submitted
a piece on the
architecture
of the Paris
Collections,
an attack on
the exhausted
quest
for the
materially
immutable which
apparently even
"forward-
thinking"
architects
are loath
to abandon.*

living in small family units, it began to
crumble when survival needs brought two
or more such self-contained clans into
repeated contact.

In perfecting the universal diagram system as a reality machine-cum-sensory
screen, the most essential factor is universal recognition, the complete acceptance of the diagram by everybody to
whom the system extends the perceptual
franchise. Without this acknowledgment,
who can be absolutely certain that the
interpretational system is absolute? And
you have to believe it is absolute, you
have to take for granted that it is absolute, because this is the reason for
having such a system in the first place:
to set a standard for measuring and thus
containing all known experience. Without
universal recognition the standard is
threatened with exposure as an arbitrary
load of rubbish, an event which would
cancel out all meaning attached to the
think margin of experience that the
screen allows to pass, thus exploding
all the definitions of reality on which
the screen itself is founded. A system

NEW YORK STREETS
FULL OF CASTOFF
VENETIAN BLINDS
THE YEAR THEY
WENT OUT OF
FASHION.

"One of the
most lovely and
inspiring
experiences to
which every
diligent student
of the Radiant
Science may
attain is contact
with the Temple
of Colour. This
is not a human or
material build-
ing, but a
degree of
consciousness....
counterpart of
this in the
physical world.

can work indefinitely providing it can
contain all the information men need to
communicate to one another in order to
stay together, and providing also that
the system does not come into contact
with another system or systems possessing
sufficient strength to recast the first
system as no more than an illusion. Some
systems were squashed by foreign invaders,
others just died of boredom. The evacua-
tion of Mayan cities need be no more
mysterious than you like. Perhaps Mayans
left for the same reason I left Philadel-
phia when I was seventeen: it was time
for a change, good or bad.

As a phenomenal universe starts falling
apart, the techniques used to sustain it
are pushed past the point where they can
do efficient work, and the same methods
which insured societal balance and order
begin to create a state of environmental
chaos. The old techniques themselves
offer no solution; the longer man re-
frains from abandoning them, the greater
the chaos. The only escape is to find
new and relatively more abstract techniques, which will raise communication to

a higher level, thus invalidating the symbolic importance attached to all previous information which has reached the cul-de-sac of sensory overload.

...The temple itself
is entirely
screened by a
crescent of tall,
beautiful trees,
whose green
radiations
at once inspire
a feeling of
harmony and
tranquility.
In front of
the magnificent
building lies
an oval lake
which reflects
like a
magnificent
mirror the
whole scene of
exquisite
splendour.
The temple is
cruciform
in shape,
and is crowned
by a large
golden dome,
with a slender
tapering spire
of glistening
white,
which symbolizes
the
Great White Light
of the
Eternal Logos.

It requires no great stretch of the imagination to see how the intensely personal quality of the olfactory system of space conditioning (which wafts back into the modern room in the form of embarrassment every time somebody farts) made it highly impractical as a method of supporting the illusion that all men in the known world were living in equal harmony with the same universe. The sensory acuteness which enabled men to move in a continuous passage of perpetual home lost its flexibility in the shock of continual intertribal interface. The barriers to communcation were too many. To overcome inevitable conflict, a new, more abstract universe, containing and invalidating all previous universal techniques, had to be devised. The sense of hearing offered a potential resolution, the perceptual door to an entirely new universe. All human-occupied space could be articulated by methods of sonic vibration, such as

music and speech. Soon human memory
would begin, the memory which recalled
that "In the beginning was the Word."

The story of the Tower of Babel is not
about the creation of world languages but
about the breakdown of the auditory universe which occurred when, during the
next series of cultural interfaces, people
found out that so many different systems
of sonic articulation existed that no
special one of them could be truly universal; they were all exposed as equally
artificial.

The four main
divisions of
the Temple
are curved and
rounded in shape,
and shine with
a brilliant
radiance,
the curves
of the
roof arches and
windows
flow and join
together
in perfect
proportion.
The entire
edifice
shines and glows
with living
Colour -
one unconsciously
absorbs /
the vital
health-giving
vibrations.
Unlike earth
buildings,
there is no
impression of
materiality
whatever
in the
construction -

The Mesopotamian ziggurat world-tower was
the symbol of the integration of man with
universe; the Tower of Babel story des-
cribes how failure to abandon the old
aural techniques prevented men from continuing with this integration process.
Instead, these methods combined to produce a total cultural breakdown, a sensory
block of sonic chaos. Media that had been
developed because of their transcendental
qualities were no longer abstract but
produced very real barriers to communica-

tion. Dependence on the word, the magical
word which had held men together, now
kept them apart. No one aural system was
strong enough to contain all the others,
and Benjamin Whorf was not yet on hand
to offer the reassurance that <u>any</u> language is good for what it is good for. It
was time for a new semiotic synthesis.

Architecture is no more than the symbolic
translation of techniques that, in previous environmental systems, had been
entirely taken for granted: of course
men needed shelter, even beavers could
build dams, spiders spin webs, and ants
construct cities. But for the new system
developed to synthesize explosions of information that could be contained no
other way, it was essential to have a
method for fixing the new abstract concepts in terms of static visuals so that
people could stop relying on the old,
outmoded techniques by investing symbolic
energy in the creation of new ones.
Architecture was developed into a language for conferring the illusion of
permanent value upon such concepts by

it is as though
the Divine
Architect
had assembled
together
the opalescent
mists and color-
ing of a
summer sunset.
From the
front view
of the
building
one sees seven
graceful
minarets
tapering
upwards, each
representing
one of the
Seven Great
Rays....
Within the
glorious
building
the same sublime
beauty is
manifested...."

-S.G.J. Ouseley,
Colour
Meditations

CIVILIZATION AS
ELABORATELY
DEVISED
SENSORY
DEPRIVATION
CHAMBER.
WE WANT
EVERYTHING
TO BE AS BORING
AS POSSIBLE
ON AS MANY
LEVELS AS
POSSIBLE.
THIS IS KNOWN
AS
TOTAL
COMMUNICATION.

The infant
Frank
Lloyd Wright
playing with
Froebel blocks -
just what
grown-up
architects do,
necessarily
embellished
with talk and
intentions,
of course.

setting up spatial diagrams that were
plainly visible to the eye.

One of the most important concepts spun
off by the transition to a visual universe was the concept of time. Time was
no more than the cerebral synthesis of an
overwhelming body of ostensibly orderless
visual information (the apparent motions
of sun, moon, planets, and stars, witnessed from a "fixed" point of view).
Stonehenge was built to give graphic substance to the necessary illusion of an
order amongst all those turning lights,
to fix the time-symbol synthesis in
visual, spatial, permanent, absolute
terms. Art historians have had a hard
time fitting Stonehenge into the aesthetic continuum, for it was built when the
visual universe was relatively raw and
unexplored. To visualize was necessary,
not merely nice: there was not yet time
for such refined embellishments as flut-
ing and entasis. Later, when the visual
universe was well established, when
visual patterns had filtered down to all
levels of experience, time was taken for

*In the universe
of motion
by credit-card
transport,
architecture
is the
poor man's
environment.*

granted, and there was no need for the
support of such an absurdly outsize mon-
ument. Soon the meaning of this corner-
stone mandala of the visual universe was
lost behind the weeds.

It should not seem so outrageous to suggest that the Great Pyramid was built at
the precise geographic center of the
earth, for it was the mathematically elegant truth of this fact that made the
pyramid a meaningful thing to do. Since
this site was the center of the universe
as well, it was no great sacrifice for
men to give up their lives for the privilege of occupying so splendid a position.
But as it is the business of civilization
not merely to maintain a fixed status
quo but to be constantly in the process
of drawing order from chaos, the static
simplicity of the Egyptian cosmos precipitated its own destruction. Having
planted the pyramid precisely and permanently and invested all energy in its
perfection, there was no energy left
over to cope with the enormous problems
brought on by the state of inertia. The

riddle was answered. The answer was correct - now what do we do? The sphinx had run out of questions.

The ancient Chinese lived and worked in the "Central Flowery People's Nation," and they cultivated the garden with the energy derived from the belief that they were central, that the garden and the world were one and the same. But when the existence of other forms of equally potent cultural behavior was revealed, by Tartars or whatever, this primal energy source was wiped out. It was impossible to go on with the great work of transforming the world into a yin-yang landscape, because the work no longer took place at the universal vortex. There were as many such centers as there were population groups to believe in them. There were also populations that got on very well without a fixed vortex at all. (Gypsies have perennial appeal because their universal style is to laugh at all the others.) So they finished the great work up as best they could under such demoralizing circumstances and put a frame around it to acknowledge its com-

FIRST WRITTEN LEGAL/ETHICAL CODE (HAMMURABI'S) LISTED PUNISHMENT FOR BUILDERS WHOSE HOUSES FELL DOWN, AND SEVERE PUNISHMENT FOR BUILDERS WHOSE HOUSES FELL DOWN AND KILLED PEOPLE, BUT, SO FAR AS IS KNOWN, CONTAINED NO AESTHETIC REQUIREMENTS FOR ARCHITECTURE - VS. THE CONTEMPORARY PICTURE:

94

FINE ARTS
COMMISSIONS
TO REGULATE
STREET FACADES,
NO LAWS TO HOLD
BUILDERS
RESPONSIBLE FOR
TENEMENTS
COLLAPSING
(ROMAN POINT
DISASTER).
BUILDING CODES
HAVING
AN EFFECT
MAINLY ON
AESTHETICS.
INCENTIVE
ZONINGS:
CONVERTING
CITIES INTO
BUSBY BERKELY
NOSTALGIC
CUT-RATE
SPECTACULARS
OF WHEN
EVERYONE WANTED
TO LIVE THERE.

pletion, a frame later known as the
Great Wall of China.

We are pleased to claim the Greeks as
cultural ancestors because they were the
first civilized real estate agents.
Greece was the first full-scale civilization to abandon the ancient whole earth/
whole universe environmental philosophy
in favor of a new, more flexible system
which let them fracture the spatial continuum into a more workable set of sub-
divisions, some of which had more development potential than others (as sacred
spots and so on). Thus they were able to
contain the information (that there was
no inherently unique earthly universal
vortex) that had undermined previous cultures. The price of this achievement was
formal specialization. Not only were some
spaces more special than others, but men's
work had to become increasingly specialized to permit successful processing of
increasing amounts of visual information
to continue. The Greeks laid a great deal
of emotional stress on the concept of the
well-rounded individual, because in the
Greek universal system such well-round-

"Le Corbusier's
Chandigarh
is currently
administered
by three
governmental
bodies,
and no one
appears to know
who owns
the city.
All future
planning
is either
ineffective,
disjointed,
or uncoordinated;
slums have
sprung up
in the center
of town
(after only
a dozen years
or so!);
large unbuilt
areas in the
center of town
are turning
into jungles.

edness was completely beyond the pale
and could be contained only as an ideal.
Plato himself mourned the loss of the old
auditory systems (just as McLuhan does
in his hymns to James Joyce). But the
Greeks had already converted music into
concert format - with stars, spectators,
and applause. Greek architects were highly specialized visual virtuosi. They had
to make buildings beautiful to conceal
the fact that they were nowhere. If
Athens could not be the center of the
universal universe, it could at least
become the vortex of an abstract universe
of synthetic beauty devised by specialized
geometers; hence the origins of the
visual aesthetic to which Western architecture has traditionally confined itself.

Later on, in Rome in the year 1, Vitruvius, molding the academic image of the
Western architect-god, held fast to the
old Greek liberal education ideal in his
advice that the prospective architect
should synthesize the talents of drafts-
man, mathematician, historian, astronomer,
writer, doctor, musician, etc., but of
course all this résumé was entirely super-

fluous. The important thing was that the architect just _act_ like God, as Dinocrates had three centuries earlier when he got the job of chief architect of the Macedonian empire by donning a chaplet of poplar leaves and presenting himself nude and oiled to Alexander the Great; or as Caesar himself did when, through travel, vision, and conquest, he set the Roman universal style so completely that for a while at least all roads led to Rome.

Gothic cathedrals were built after Jesus Christ had for various political reasons become universally accepted as the world's salvation. Later, when the secular quest for knowledge threatened to reveal the beauty of other gods, it was necessary to become evangelistic in order to preserve this universality intact. If everybody wasn't convinced that Christ saved the world, then eating bread and wine in Holy Communion would be absurd and insane. Those who weren't Christian had to be scientifically certified genetically backward, and either converted, massacred, or condemned to limbo. It was still, of course, possible to build

One expects that, should Chandigarh, through some totally unforeseeable sequence of events, ever evolve into a town, someone will be on hand to declare it a testament to Corb's genius, his acumen, his foresight.

IRAN SEEKS $30,000,000 to TO REBUILD BABYLON "ACCORDING TO ITS ORIGINAL ARCHITECTURAL DESIGNS"; CREEPING VEGETATION AND WAR IN SOUTHEAST ASIA THREATEN TO DESTROY ANGKOR WAT.

cathedrals, but they could no longer serve as universal energy reservoirs, except perhaps on Sunday mornings. The rest of the week they had to earn their keep as museums.

Universal Renaissance man took a few steps backward to get a better view, and fell clear out of the visual universe. The earth, it soon appeared, was not even the center of the local light show. Disintegration of the visual platform begins with perspective techniques which created perceptual consciousness as a thing apart (thereby increasing the need for philosophic methods, such as humanism, to complete the universal hologram with man inside).

Since the early Renaissance, architecture could do no more than provide a witty trompe l'oeil denouement. Later, Leonardo had a vision of the helix dangling beyond the visual vanishing point, was so wrecked by this that he started writing backwards. He had to keep his insights on an arcane level because there was obviously a lot more visual computation (sight leading to insight) required before the precise nature of the next step could be revealed, through Einstein, in abstract universal terms. Leonardo knew but couldn't tell. L.H.O. aux yeux is the secret of Mona Lisa's smile.

TO BUILD WALLS, TO BLOW THEM UP: WHICH IS THE MORE HUMANITAR- IAN GESTURE? IT'S ALL PART OF THE SAME REPETITIOUS ROUTINE. I DUMP MY BLUEPRINTS IN A PHONE BOOTH AT THE GARE DU NORD - FREEDOM: BEING ABLE TO WALK OUT OF OTHER PEOPLE'S FREEDOM WITH A LIGHT HEART, WITHOUT LOOKING BACK. WALKING THROUGH WALLS SOME NEED TO SURVIVE. LIGHTS COME ON AT THE TOP OF THE TOUR EIFFEL, A MONTH'S REST AT 66 BOULEVARD EXELMANS, I START WRITING.

They suppressed Galileo, and when that failed they built Versailles. But not even Newton could maintain the credibili- ty of the fixed mundane vortex: attempts to restore it were soon overthrown by the mob and/or laid to rest in some museum. The Industrial Revolution was an arbitrary date set for stepping up the rate of withdrawal from the visual uni- verse. Architects liked it no better than the Luddites, but by the nineteenth century - William Morris notwithstanding - it had become the business of archi- tecture to generate as much environmental chaos as possible, to create a visual theater of the absurd. Babel was back, this time in more explicitly architec- tural form.

The purpose of the international style of modern architecture, especially as crys-

ROOM TO LET.
LIVING ANYWHERE,
LIKE OUR GHORFA
ON THE EDGE
OF THE SAHARA.
SETTLING BACK
WITH OUR BLANKETS
AND TRANSISTORS
INTO DIRT
WHICH HAS
EVERY RIGHT
TO EXPRESS ITSELF
OR, RATHER,
TO BE WITNESSED;
SINCE IT IS
SUCH A
FUNDAMENTAL
EXPRESSION OF
LIVING BEINGS.
DIRT:
A GREAT
CONNECTION
BETWEEN "MAN"
AND
"HIS ENVIRONMENT,"
IF ONE IS
NEEDED.
DUST TO DUST,
AND ALL THAT.
MODERN
ARCHITECTURE IS
SO VICTORIAN-
PRUDISH;
CONCRETE NETHER
GARMENTS
TO SHROUD
THE WORLD'S LAST
REMAINING
EROGENOUS ZONES

tallized in the classic work of Mies, was
to give us a final perfect glimpse of the
Euclidean universe from which we had all
been preparing to depart for four centuries. In its semitransparent celebra-
tion of the plane it sums up the aesthetic adventure of three thousand years in
a spatial event bidding final farewell
to a universe styled on the structural
properties of trees for the latter-day
descendants of tree-dwellers. The Seagram
Building is a suitably dignified memorial
to time-honored space, passing.

From the old spatial point of view, as
nobody needs Peter Blake and the bathos
brigade of urban garbage photographers
to remind him, everything is indeed a
mess. The last remaining duty of a collapsing phenomenal universe is to appear
as hopelessly catastrophic as possible.
In the case of the visual universe, an
intolerable degree of ugliness is only to
be expected. The environment is polluted
for the same reason that the novel is
"dead" and pornography is legalized. The
only vital visual expressions left are
those that show what has never before

(A CHRISTO
EMPAQUETAGE
GONE WILD,
TAKEN TOO
SERIOUSLY).
MUD-BAKED GHORFA,
AN ARCHITECTURE
REQUIRING
NO MAIDS OR
ELECTRONIC
HELPERS.
CLEANLINESS
OBSESSION:
RATIONAL DESIRE
TO SEPARATE
MEN FROM OTHER
PHENOMENA.

Bed/sit.
Incredible
how many people
consent
to live this way
in London.
You may sit up
to drink tea,
read the paper,
watch telly,
talk to friends
(not too loudly).
You may lie down
to go to bed.
All other
postures
explicitly
forbidden.
Bed/sit.

been shown: Technicolor nonidealized
nudes, chrome-yellow Los Angeles sunsets,
the destruction of wildlife, the glori-
fied soup can - everything, as the visual
screen breaks down. New York is a culture
capital not because the best artists live
there but because the quickest critics
do, men whose business is to collect and
sort all visual images and file them
away with or without editorial comment.
All systems perceived through the visual
sense - astronomy, astrology, chemistry,
alchemy, science, art - are perceived as
equally valid for what they do.

Attempts at "beautification" through the
visual sense (replacing slums with de-
lightful malls, trashing city streets
with tulips and ginkgoes) will result in
a proportionate increase of visual chaos,
just as efforts toward enforced environmental security (locks, gates, vaults,
guards) will be met by equal forces of
threat to this security. The "best" buildings, the "most beautiful" streets are
bogus gestures that make everything seem
even more chaotic by preventing us from
fully accepting and acting upon the fact

101

that the old space is dead, that we no
longer believe in the power of straight
lines, fixed angles, corners, shapes, and
space packages of _any_ kind to have a
significant effect on our experience.
Such architecture continues to exist in
precisely the same way other supersti-
tions, like knocking on wood, do. Fixed
habitats, well-designed exteriors and interiors, lovely homes, and fair cities
have become museums of unnatural history,
faded tableaux that demonstrate the failure of the design process to match wits
with the new dimensions. The old environmental cues become quaint throwbacks de-
void of original intended meaning - like
a medieval astrolabe, once key to the
universal diagram, now on display at the
notion counter as a decorator-touch paper-
weight.

As the nova phase of the visual universe
draws to an epic fade-out, through which
sense, if any, will a new system come
into play? It is doubtful that McLuhan's
attempt to revive the ear will be much
more successful than Mike Todd Jr.'s bid

How the New York
boardinghouses
for struggling
would-be
Broadway stars
in thirties
movies are so
huge and
beautiful, yet
the heroine
turns to her
soon-to-be beau
and, embarrassed,
says, "well,
this is it...."

102

for the nose was back in the fifties with
Smell-O-Vision. Nothing can resuscitate
phenomena whose time has passed, except
in novel entertainment form. It is
through the undeveloped sense (which, in
its very haziness, seems to promise new
and better forms of communication) that
new universal systems are synthesized
from the experience that cannot be contained within the old.

In Berlin, at turn of the century,
Gordon Craig and Isadora Duncan became
lovers. It was a symbolic interface.
Craig affected the modern cause, Duncan
claimed empathy with the ancients;
nevertheless hers was the world to come,
his the universe passing. He was the
stubborn persistence of vision, she
the moving object for whom vision had
become a secondary attribute. As they
walked the streets together, transforming pedestrian strassen into dynastic
professional avenues, they shared the
kinetic experience. Then, while Craig
darted back to his stationary drawing
table, Duncan continued the walk.

LEARNING
TO SEND OUT
INVULNERABILITY
VIBES
WHILE LIVING ON
SEVENTH STREET
BETWEEN B AND C.
ARCHITECTURE
AS EXPRESSION
OF FEAR.
FEAR OF
NOT BELONGING,
OR GOING CRAZY,
OF THE WORLD
COMING
TO AN END,
OF GOING TO HELL.
THE PRISON:
THAT THE
MOST PERFECTLY
CRYSTALLINE FORM
OF SPACE-TIME
SHOULD AMOUNT
TO A MUSEUM
OF "SOCIALLY
ABERRANT
BEHAVIOR."

MEANING BACK TO
THE MOST BASIC...
TO CONNECT
THE FOUR SQUARES
OF THIS ROOM
TO WHAT I KNOW
AND HAVE YET TO
UNDERSTAND
(GUILT OVER SUCH
TRIVIAL NEGATIVE
COMMENTS ABOUT
OTHER PEOPLE'S
WORK)
...THE THINGS
THAT ARE HOLDING
THE ROOF UP,
LETTING THE
LIGHT IN,
KEEPING THE WIND
OUT;
THE UNITY
DWELLING
THROUGH ME IN ALL
THE DETAILS....
THE NECESSARY
AND DESIRABLE
CRUDENESS OF
ONE'S SHELTER,
ONE'S LANGUAGE,
AMERICAN INDIAN
MODEL:
NO NEED FOR
ARCHITECTURE
BY A PEOPLE WHOSE
LANGUAGE CONTAINS
NO WORD FOR WHY...
RITUAL VIGIL
TO KEEP THE WORLD
WORKING,

In transcribing the experience into visual terms, Craig previewed a theatrical
version of the modern movement's coming
monster design of total dictatorship in
which expression of individual being was
forbidden. Duncan had no fixed base, no
environmental fixes apart from the famous
blue curtains she could hang anywhere she
happened to be. She founded no school,
invented no original dance gestures,
because her language was universal - her
method, to do what everyone does but to
be aware what one is doing.

Craig's work was confined to the theater,
and even so it was not Craig but D.W.
Griffith who finally realized the former's
dream of the actor as ..."über-marion-
ette...." While Craig labored away at flat
illusions of worlds on the other side of
the proscenium, Duncan was teaching her-
self to wear space by investing her
simplest movements with symbolism, and she
used this refined kinesthetic sense to
design a continuous four-dimensional
passage from San Francisco to La Gloire.
Her language made the design of a setting
superfluous; the spatial continuum itself

THE SUN
IN THE SKY,
THROUGH
EXPERIENCING
THIS EXPERIENCE
WHICH IS NOT,
STRICTLY
PERCEIVED.
SUNLIGHT
CAST ON THE FLOOR
IN A SQUARE,
THE LITTLE
TRIANGLES
OF WOOD THAT
HOLD UP THE
SHELVES,
REGULAR
AND CHANCE
SHAPES;
TREES OUTSIDE
THE WINDOW
AND FURTHER,
ACROSS
THE STREET,
CLOUDS
...THE
ARCHITECTURE
OF LATE NIGHTS,
COFFEE STAINS,
CIGARETTE BUTTS...
WEALTH
WITHOUT DESIGN...
CONTROL
ONLY BY REFUSAL
TO SEPARATE
THINGS...
THAT THE
RATIONAL FULLER
DEFINITION OF
THINKING
(BUCKY'S BAD
EYESIGHT
MADE HIM OVERLY
VISUAL,

was her mise-en-scène. A year before
Einstein published his general theory of
relativity, Duncan lifted her arms in the
portal of the Parthenon and opened the
doors to the kinesthetic universe.

If there is such a thing as kinesthetic
architecture, it is no more than the
symbolic translation of techniques which,
in the mainstream of Western civilization,
have been either entirely taken for
granted (of course men can walk, horses
gallop, seagulls fly) or else reserved
for vastly heroic undertakings (Moses
parting the Red Sea, the Ark, the Trojan
Horse, Hannibal crossing the Alps,
Cleopatra's barge, the Allied liberation
of Paris, lunar landings). Hyperdevelop-
ment of kinesthetic techniques by industry insured accelerated removal of symbolism from visual levels and its invest-
ment in every form of perceptible motion
- manual, mechanical, cerebral. Primary
energy attached to wall, picture, written
word, is dispersed. Still life is parody.
Environment becomes a perpetual-motion
machine at the disposal of individual
consciousness, not some grand external to

TOOK HIM BACK
TO THE STAGE OF
EIGHTEENTH-
CENTURY
RATIONAL
RETREAT FROM
VISUAL,
WHEREAS THE
CULTURAL MILIEU
FOR WHICH
HE DESIGNS
HAS ALREADY
PROGRESSED
TO THE
INTUITIVE)
AS "MOMENTARY
DISMISSAL OF
IRRELEVANCIES"
...WHEREAS
ALL IS EQUALLY
IRRELEVANT,
EVERYTHING
CAN BE PROVED,
AND THAT KIND
OF THINKING
IS MORE AND
MORE BORING,
OK,
YOU'VE PROVED
THAT ONE;
NEXT....

be grandly designed by fictionalized im-
personal agencies such as Newton's God
and Fuller's freeze-dried ephemeris.

"In the end," wrote Marcel Breuer, "we
shall sit on resilient cushions of air,"
but through Einstein we go one better:
we already sit on resilient cushions of
illusion. All architecture, from the time
someone first created the cave in the
image of home, is based on principles
scientifically operative in the technique
of holograms, or the temporary projection
of imaginary visual forms in empty space.
The building is the spatial projection of
an event taking place in space-time.
When the steady foundation of Euclid goes,
so does the collective reality which
acknowledged the inalienable right of
the building to claim an external value
superior to that of muscae volitantes or
other visual apparitions. Whether of stone,
steel, or rubber, the building begins to
lose its shape.

Fuller's comprehensive verbal ramblings
are no more capable of actually designing motion than Corb's polemic picto-

graphs of ocean liners and airplanes; at
best they merely suggest the idea of
motion, like Erich Mendelssohn's jet-
stream drawing technique. But as the
universe of motion is already upon us,
there is no need to suggest it, in the
tradition that died with Norman Bel
Geddes a few years back. While the geodesic dome and the pneumatic structure
may perhaps serve as introductory symbols to the kinesthetic universe for
those who still are primarily visually
oriented, it is clear that in a universe
of motion there can be no importance at
all attached to the structural design of
any parcel of "space" (whether a single
lot or a whole planet). No space can
possibly be any more geodesic than any
other space, because there is no space
to be articulated in any fashion; only
motion can be articulated or expressed,
by a sense which is incapable of dis-
tinguishing between some spaces and
others, because only motion is universal,
i.e., holds true for all observers. The
kinesthetic sense transforms space into
a riding habit, attire to be worn while
traveling, disposable like a paper ward-

NO SUCH THING
AS WASTE;
WASTE IS JUST
LOOKING AT
SOMETHING
OBJECTIVELY
AND NOT
UNDERSTANDING
ITS FUNCTION.

robe. Buildings in any style at all, the entire history of architecture itself, provide the moving sense with a continually varied flow of spatial appoggiatura, in contrast to the picture of visual cacophony witnessed by the eye.

Environmental awareness is shifted from the dimensions of the image to the process by which the image is projected. Environments can no longer be kept alive by pleasing shapes but by knowing or accidental articulation of the process of kinetic interchange between "observers" in relative states of motion. A building is much more interesting during construction or demolition than when it is just standing there. Without son et lumière programs, many famous works of architecture would vanish into impalpable air. The average U.S. homeowner, who moves every two and a half years, is a practiced hologrammer. The average U.S. home is just a cardboard annex to a two-car garage. The car provides a dramatic demonstration of the way in which an individual warps the environment around himself into a perceptual world wholly be-

Feng-shui: System used by the ancient Chinese to determine the correct articulation of the geographical spatial continuum, where to put buildings, towns, bridges, what kind of buildings, forms, materials, etc. No subdivision. Compare with a personalized architecture of the intuitive, a polymorphous architecture, transforming through the brief accentuation rather than imposition. (Wright almost tried this, but wouldn't give up the "beyond implications" of his design;

tradition
reduced to
absurdity
by Soleri –
using Ecojargon
to cloak an
environmental
statement
considerably
less advanced,
ecologically
speaking,
than the
honest squalor
of
ancient Rome.)

*Using candles,
rooms,
books,
noises,
advice,
haircuts,
incense,
oranges,
whatever
you need to keep
yourself in touch
with the touch
for calling forth
home
from the endless
presence
of absolute,
universal
everything.*

yond the grasp of the drawing board but immediately responsive to his ability to regulate the flow of kinetic energy. Like car stereo, Glorious Living Space envelops you everywhere you go. The Euclidean universe provides a temporary free parking lot for the kinesthetic. In the megapolitan kinematic, the town has come to circus.

Communication emphasis shifts from expression as product to expression as the perpetual "act or process of pressing out" energy, in any form, or in no form. The function of the artifact is simply to provide a pretext, for those who need one, to get out there to "places" (streets, galleries, theaters, schools, laundromats, shopping centers) where they can feel free to move around. The painting on display is secondary: the opening is all that counts. Standard architecture provides waiting rooms for those whose time to boogie has not yet arrived. Books and magazines and television provide temporary means of transport. Everybody is a visionary architect all the time, without even trying.

AMERICAN INDIAN
MODEL:
RITUAL
RENEWAL OF
LIVING SPACE.
A PEOPLE
WHOSE LANGUAGE
CONTAINS
NO WORD WHY
WOULD PROBABLY
BE LESS
INTERESTED IN
ARCHITECTURE
THAN A PEOPLE
FOR WHOM
SUCH A WORD
IS CONSIDERED
TERRIFICALLY
PROFOUND.

The visual stereotypes can no longer be
taken seriously. The environmental cues
of the good life are perceived as anal
compulsive stumbling blocks, to be kicked
aside or used imaginatively in environmental situation comedy. The female, the
black, all beings classed as objects in
the visual catalog, explode with kinetic
techniques to demonstrate their equal
energy. The classified schizophrenic (the
shaman/clown of all phenomenal universes),
who has made a career of mocking the lifeless uniformity of the visual life by
assuming exaggerated postures of stasis
(catatonia, melancholia, the strait
jacket), is recognized as a cultural pre-
mutant, a troubadour of kinesthesia, a
being who required no Einstein to understand that the illusions of space and
time are ultimate restrictions against
communication.

Not just buildings, but all material
packages begin to assume strange new
appearances. On TV (which - media experts
to the contrary - is less a causal factor
of the kinesthetic gestalt than an early
monitor of its existence), politicians

110

Victor Hugo
as
polymorphous
architect
of
Notre Dame.

*Duchamp's
chess boards
as scale
models of
kinesthetic
architecture.*

and talk-show celebrities must use make-
up and special lighting not just - as in
movies - to take on a different visual
package from one's own, but merely to
hold together the parts of the visual
gestalt before the scrutiny of the TV
kinematic; to retain intact, in other
words, the image of themselves which they
wear with equanimity in the "normal"
world still operating on yet-to-be-
devalued visual currency. Gradually, the
ideal human form mocked up by the Greeks
and culminating in the industrial design
mean specimen of Dreyfuss and others,
becomes less and less relevant as a symbolic reference of what human beings are
taken to be, a transitional process well
depicted in Picasso's Demoiselles d'Avig-
non. "Primitive" images have the appearance they do, not because of ignorance
or limited techniques of craftsmanship,
but because that is the way people look
to people who look that way at people,
people who take for granted that people
know what other people look like. "I am
a visual man," wrote Le Corbusier, "and
this makes true architecture." We need
not concern ourselves too much, there-

fore, with the future of true architecture.

Architecture is a word whose Greek etymon means "that which is above tecture," i.e., above mere building or construction. Formerly it was possible for a building to be architecture because the existence of a reality above "space" itself was unknown. But when absolute space ceases to be universal, construction is unable to transcend itself and architecture, almost by definition, becomes the work of men whose business has nothing whatever to do with construction. The Bauhaus sprang up in recognition of this fact, but it got carried away in high art interpretations twice again removed from where architecture, true or false, was actually happening. In the famous "Two Cultures" period it was the dream of the artist/designer to be the one to bring the magic human touch to the cold workings of industrial technology. The Gropius legacy of "taming technology" lives on in contemporary architecture schools where students, disillusioned by the irrelevancy of the archaic building

ALICE AND I
ARE SHOVED
BACK
ON BOARD
ONCE MORE
BY MEMORY:
ALL IS
AS IT SHOULD
BE.

112

parcels they still have to do to qualify as certified architects, turn to making multi-media "process" designs for the "optimization" of existing environmental facilities without the use of design/construction. While showing a healthy bid for cultural relevance often lacking in architecture, the attempt of the drawing board to outpace or even keep up with trends in commercial industry is not unlike the fatuous attempt of haute couture to contain the "death of fashion" by presenting Levi Strauss with the Coty Award. The process designs do no more than provide trendy architecture magazines with trendy 2-D duplications of systems which, if not already in commercially successful operation, are being constructively prepared by businessmen who have no need to prove their cultural relevance. "The specialized persons who make up the world of industry and business live, therefore, in this virile atmosphere where indubitably lovely works are created," wrote Corb, longing for an excitement he could never achieve in his own field. The architecture of Robert Venturi springs from his longing to be

113

the young Bob Dylan, racing down the
highway on his bike, making poetry out
of Desolation Row.

Fuller steps in where Gropius left off,
closing the science/humanities gap in his
own mind by exalting himself as a compre-
hensivist while jet-setting round the
globe in planes made possible by the work
of the anonymous specialists from whom
he scornfully grabs the credit. Oskar
Schlemmer, who eschewed this treadmill
run after technology, emerges as the most
interesting of the Bauhaus artists. Lim-
iting himself to what he could do on the
spot with a handful of props and applied
information, he was the only major
Bauhaus figure to devote himself exclusively to kinesthetic research while the
others, even Moholy-Nagy, were still
bogged down in panvisuals. Perhaps if
Fuller came off his totally yin-free diet
of steak and orange juice, he might worry
less about gaps and see clear to perfecting his own valuable (and highly specialized) contribution to the art of the
global dancer.

I call
this book
a monograph
because
it's less an
ideological
statement
than a typed
transcript
of what
I have been
doing
for a while to
"condition my
environment";
I've been
writing a book
about
architecture.
I have created
architecture
in the image
of a maze
to give myself
practice in the
art of
escaping
mazes.

At last,
there are no
olfactory,
auditory,
visual,
kinesthetic,
parapsychologi-
cal,
rational,
or intuitive
universes.
All this is
speciousness
I am glad
to be done with
for a while.
The writing
has suddenly
become a maze,
so I stop
this book
with a smile
instead
of a
forecast.

THERE
Could it be
a cock and bull
story?
Oakland
Makes It There

Thomas Albright

In one of those "conceptual art" capers
that manage to dovetail beautifully into
an old-fashioned publicity stunt, a ceramic "there" was formally presented this
week to Oakland's Mayor John H. Reading.

The Mayor listened graciously as artist
Tom Zimmerman explained that the "there"
was being presented to observe the 99th
birthday of Gertrude Stein, who was
reared in the East Bay City and who later
declared - in one of her few comprehensi-
ble statements - "there is no there
there."

Zimmerman, a San Francisco photographer,
claimed to have found the ceramic piece
- with its "t" inexplicably backwards -
in the palatial home of a Central American coffee planter who "deals in clan-
destine art works," after having first
purchased a "fake" "there" on a parchment
scroll from a man he met wandering around
the jungle. Zimmerman said he was simply
returning a "there" to Oakland which had
just been missing for all these years.

116

"That sounds like a cock and bull story
to me," Mayor Reading said, but he proceeded to thank Zimmerman for his "gen-
erous gift" and delivered a prepared talk
outlining Oakland's efforts to produce
"a real and very unique 'there' here."

He cited the symphony, museum, port,
sports and entertainment attractions,
and said "I think that if Miss Stein were
alive and with us today she most certainly would agree with you that there is
indeed a 'there' here."

Before the presentation, there was some
talk among museum officials, reporters
and others gathered in the Mayor's office
of far-reaching implications for the symbolic gift, like renaming the City
"there" and erecting the word in giant
lights over Oakland's airport. None of
these were officially advanced to the
Mayor, but he did promise that the gift
would be conspicuously displayed in the
City Hall foyer.

-San Francisco
Chronicle,
February 3, 1973.